RITUAL AND DRAMA

RITUAL AND DRAMA

THE MEDIAEVAL THEATRE

Francis Edwards

With line drawings by
George Tuckwell

Distributed Exclusively By

INTERNATIONAL IDEAS INC.
1627 Spruce Street
Philadelphia PA USA 19103

LUTTERWORTH PRESS
GUILDFORD AND LONDON

First published 1976

The author and the publishers wish to thank the British Library Board for permission to reproduce photographs of the Holkham Picture Bible; together with the incumbents of the churches of Worth in Sussex, Kilpeck in Herefordshire, Iver in Buckinghamshire, St Laurence's in Ludlow, Shropshire, and Hexham Abbey, Northumberland, for their kind permission to reproduce photographs of their churches.

Plates 1, 5, 6 and 7 were taken by Morgan-Wells: Plates 2A, 2B, 2C, 3A, 3B, 4A, 4B, and 8 were taken by the author.

Filmset and printed Offset Litho in Great Britain by Cox & Wyman Ltd, London, Fakenham and Reading

CONTENTS

Note: the monochrome plates appear between pages 64 and 65.

TO
THE
SURREY
COMMUNITY
PLAYERS

PREFACE

In this book I have endeavoured to trace and discuss in non-academic terms the emergence of the mediaeval play from Christian ritual. In other words, the book is frankly addressed to young students and general readers whose interest in the mediaeval theatre has been newly aroused. In writing it I have tried consistently to bear in mind the difficulties which beset those students, of whom there are many, whose contact with the Christian faith is, to say the least, tenuous, and for whom in consequence the liturgy of the Church is a closed book. It is to be hoped that I have dealt with the subject in such a way that the modern reader is able to view the emergence of drama from religious ritual in a completely detached way, as a common human phenomenon which he may compare, if he wishes, with the classical example of the Greek theatre.

In choosing to limit the subject to the period extending from the tenth century to the end of the fifteenth I was moved by the wish to encourage in the reader's mind a sense of the integrity of the mediaeval theatre in its rise and eventual decline. The student, therefore, who wishes to bridge the gap between the mediaeval and Elizabethan periods, will need to consult other and more compendious works which cover the Tudor theatre. Very much the same explanation must be given for my neglect of the mediaeval folk drama, the relevance of which, in view of the present state of our knowledge, must be open to question. I have, nevertheless, tried to give due weight to the survival of pagan habits of mind in mediaeval audiences, in attempting to assess the probable impact upon them of Christian ritual and dramatic stress.

I should like to acknowledge in the warmest terms the generous help given to me by Mrs I. M. McNeill who has brought to bear the wealth of her experience as a headmistress in vetting the text for me. My thanks are also due to my friend and colleague, Mr Joseph Hill, for much kindly advice in whatever photography I have supplied, and above all for producing the prints, at times performing miracles with negatives of uncertain merit.

Francis Edwards
Reigate, 1976

1

RITUAL AND THE
THEATRE

Any book that deals with the history of the theatre must begin with a reference to ritual. This is because ritual of one sort or another forms the basis of all popular theatrical entertainment and the root from which the dramatic art itself has grown. How this is so, and how it applies to the theatre and drama of Mediaeval Europe, I shall try to explain in this chapter: and because it is always better when we are thinking about the past to clarify our ideas about the present, let us start with an examination of a highly popular modern ritual which bears a strong relationship to theatrical entertainment.

Consider, then, the sort of happening that can be seen taking place on the terraces of any of the major football grounds while a match is in progress. Grouped together in order that their voices may be heard in concert we find a number of spectators, usually members of a 'supporters' club', who chant, clap their hands, display coloured scarves, and sometimes even dance in their efforts to urge or 'will' their favoured football side on to victory. Their club, it is important to remember, is engaged in a conflict in which *Chance* in the shape of the current form of the opposing teams, the weather conditions, which may be more suitable to one side than the other, and even the decisions of the referee and the two linesmen, plays a very important part. What is also significant is the fact that these same supporters associate themselves so closely with their football club that they tend to think of the team selected by the club manager not so much in terms of 'them' as of 'us'.

Now let us consider, in a perfectly detached way, the behaviour of these groups of supporters. This is always more or less of a pattern, so that were it not for the words chanted, and the colours

or 'favours' worn by the members of each group, it would be difficult to distinguish one from another. In the first place, they all
chant together, which means that they form a chorus. Secondly,
their chant is rhythmical and frequently preceded by the clapping
of hands, with the rhythm of the latter anticipating the rhythm of
the chant itself. Here is a typical example which any football
enthusiast will recognize:

Clapping u   –   u   –   –

Chant   We are the champions.

Besides this, in moments of joy, usually when their side scores a
goal, they dance vigorously while those of their group who carry
coloured scarves hold them stretched above their heads to
signify their triumph.

We call this behaviour a ritual because it takes place on a
special occasion and because it conforms to a pattern which is
regulated and accepted by common consent of all who take part
in it. Not all rituals are the same, however, and we have to explain
why it is that our chosen example is of special importance to us in
this book. To begin the process, it will be helpful to make a list of
the major points already noted. These are as follows:

1   The groups are gathered together to witness a *Conflict*
between two teams of footballers in which *Chance* as well as
human skill plays a part.

2   It is the desire of each group to urge or *'Will'* one of the teams
to victory.

3   Each group forms a chanting, clapping and gesticulating
Chorus.

4   In giving form and rhythm to their chanting they fashion a
primitive kind of *Art*.

5   So closely personal is their association with their favourite
club that victory or defeat for the club's chosen team means
victory or defeat for *'Us'*.

Now, all these points add up to what is frequently described as
tribal behaviour. This is not to suggest that there is anything wrong
about such behaviour—quite the contrary, as a matter of fact.
People come from their homes, their factories and offices to 'take

time off' from the pressures and very frequently from the boredom imposed by modern society, to find release through the exercise of their basic instincts. They like the skilful conflict of football; they like the partisanship it excites; and they like the sense of 'belonging' which comes with the declared support of a football club. They are 'the faithful', and many of them are religiously so. Nevertheless, the fact remains that every one of these urges or instincts is a reminder of the far-distant past when our forefathers gathered together in communal or tribal groups to express their urgent desire for survival in what was to them the grimly *dramatic* conflict between the powers of life and death. This was a conflict in which primitive man regarded himself very much as a spectator since he had neither the skill nor the understanding to master the warring elements about him. He could do no more than urge or *Will* the outcome in his favour, and this he did by employing the same ritualistic means as those which we see in action on the terraces of the football grounds. Men gathered themselves into groups or choruses and communicated their collective will through the media of song and dance.

Now, ritual, whenever it is associated with the life and death conflict of a community, inevitably tends to become a sacred act or office. This is largely because of the need in Man to address his desires, his hopes and his fears to an intelligible being rather than to blind chance. Such a being is dignified with the name of god or goddess because he or she exercises a remote power over human destiny. Thus, as soon as men become conscious of the association of the sun's heat with the fertility of the soil, they tend to imagine the sun as a glorious male god and the earth as a mother goddess. When gods and goddesses are conceived in this way as a direct result of Man's consciousness of his absolute dependence upon the forces of nature, we say that they are pagan. This is a matter which we shall need to bear in mind, especially during the early stages of our study.

The next thing that we have to consider is the way in which the acted play or drama develops from ritual. There must, of course, always be an element of drama in ritual itself: because drama *is* conflict and ritual evolves as a result of Man's experience of the conflict of life. The art of making a play, however, seems usually to begin as soon as it becomes necessary to *demonstrate* the way in which a god, or even blind chance, acts in directing the lives of

11

men and women. For this reason the earlier and sometimes the greatest plays of a particular culture or civilization are concerned with legends which surround divine or god-like images. The ancient Greek drama ranks among these, and if you are a student of Greek as well as mediaeval theatre you will know that the art of Greek tragedy developed from the ritual dance of the *dithyramb* which was performed in honour of the god Dionysus, or Bacchus as he is often called. Nowadays we are inclined to think of Dionysus as a god of wine, but to the ancient Greeks he was much more than that. He was an agricultural god associated with the fertility of crops, and especially with the fertility of trees.

The stem from which the mediaeval theatre grew was the Christian ritual of the Mass. We shall, of course, have to consider certain details of this ritual, but before doing so it will be necessary to give some attention to the conditions surrounding the lives of mediaeval people because, as has already been pointed out, the approach of a community or a people to its religious ritual is very closely related to the conflicts involved in its struggle for survival.

Let us begin with the description given by the great Hugh Latimer of the circumstances of his boyhood, which would have been towards the end of the fifteenth century. Hugh Latimer, who was burned at the stake during the reign of Mary Tudor, gave his description in the course of a sermon which he delivered in the presence of Edward VI, and it is worth noting that he drew his picture with more than a little regret, as though he were looking back to 'better times'. This is what he had to say:

My father was a yeoman, and he had no lands of his own, only he had a farm of three or four pound by the year at the uttermost, and hereupon he tilled so much as kept half a dozen men [*in work*]. He had walk [*pasture*] for a hundred sheep; and my mother milked thirty kine. He was able, and did, find the king a harness, with himself and his horse [*could equip himself with armour, weapons and a horse, if called upon to go to war*]. . . .

I can remember that I buckled his harness when he went unto Blackheath field [*where the Cornish rebels were defeated by Henry VII's army in 1497*]. He kept me to school, or else I had not been able to preach before the king's majesty now. He married [*found husbands for*] my sisters with five pound or twenty nobles apiece [*and provided them with satisfactory dowries*] so that he brought them up in godliness and fear of God. He kept hospitality for his poor neighbours, and some alms he gave to the poor. . . .

Now, this description is exceedingly interesting, not only because of what it says, but also because of what it neglects to say. It gives us a picture of a moderately well-off yeoman or tenant farmer of the period who was not only common to the age but also the backbone of the country. Superficially it is an ideal picture — one, indeed, which might easily represent a modern country-lover's dream with its impression of a tough, tightly-knit, self-reliant household, sufficiently prosperous to be generous in sharing with others. Evidently, a household worthy of respect in its day. But now let us fill in some of the details which Latimer left out, not, let it be said, because he wished to present a distorted picture, but because to him and his audience such details would have been so commonplace and self-evident that to have named them would have been superfluous.

First, there is the matter of the armour and weapons carried by Latimer senior in the service of his king. These implements of war would not have been kept in a state of readiness simply so that they could be placed at the king's disposal. This was a brutal and savage age in which every man had to be ready either to kill or be killed in the protection of his own. Latimer's father would have needed to go armed and in company, probably even when travelling to his local town of Leicester. For all roads were dangerous and a man might easily be struck down, not necessarily by thieves and outlaws, though of these there were plenty, but in equal likelihood by enemies with a sense of personal grievance. This points to weakness in the enforcement of the law: for Latimer's father would have known his entitlement to protection from the king whom he served. But enforcement of the law was all too often in the hands of officers whose honesty and sense of duty could not be relied upon. Much would have depended upon the favour of the lord of the manor who could, and frequently did, countenance the acts of murderous ruffians who might well be in his pay.

It is in this light that we need to interpret the impression of self-reliance and close neighbourliness given by Latimer's account. Men and women were vividly conscious of living in a hostile world: and this explains one of the many sharp contrasts that exist between mediaeval life and our own. Mediaeval people were far more insular in their outlook than we, with the world-wide view of things given to us by newspapers and radio and

13

television. Throughout the mediaeval period people remained locally attached, no matter whether they lived within town or village. A London merchant, for example, travelling, say, to Norwich, could expect to be treated as a foreigner on reaching his destination, just as if he had come from Amsterdam or Cologne or Venice. In other words, and this applied throughout Europe, people were conscious of themselves and others as belonging to a certain city or town or village rather than to a country. We, as students of theatre, need to bear this 'sense of belonging' clearly in mind when we are considering the mediaeval reaction to ritual. It is of vital importance, as every football fan knows.

But the difficulties attendant upon living in a violent world would by no means have been the greatest of the Latimers' problems. Here at least the hazards would have been known and prepared for. Far more to be feared were the totally unpredictable hazards of famine and disease. And this brings us to the major feature of mediaeval life which every person interested in the theatre and drama of the period needs to understand.

First of all we have to consider the complete vulnerability of mediaeval people to the natural elements. The fruits of the earth were the hard-earned reward of sheer physical labour. People, therefore, lived very close to the soil and were in consequence intensely aware of the seasonal changes or rhythm of the year. Spring to them meant the awakening of the earth under the life-giving warmth of the sun: and its occurrence was seen as no less than a mystery and a miracle, for there was no science to interpret the universe for them as a machine. Summer, of course, was a time of plenty, while winter was a period of dearth when earth and its vegetation died, so that flocks of sheep and herds of cattle had to be killed off because there was insufficient pasture to support them. This consciousness of a majestic though terrifying rhythm was just as sharp in the towns as it was in the countryside, for there was no clear distinction between urban life and country life as there is today. A town or even a city was a small place, the population of which rarely exceeded a few thousands, and it was not uncommon at harvest-time for the apprentices to be turned out to help in the fields which surrounded the town walls.

But there were times, as now, when the rhythm failed. Spring might be late in coming after an exceptionally bitter winter; the summer might bring continuous heavy rains; or, which would be infinitely worse, there might be a cycle of unseasonable weather lasting for perhaps two or three years. The effects of such happenings would be immediate, and they would be disastrous. We know that they occurred, and we know that famine followed swiftly in their wake.

Death from disease was common: but it was epidemic disease which was most to be feared. In Hugh Latimer's time the sweating sickness seemed to be the most serious cause of terror. We do not ourselves know precisely what the sweating sickness was, though modern medical men seem to think that it was a particularly vicious and deadly kind of influenza. Even more deadly, however, was the plague which has come to be known as the Black Death. This terrible scourge struck Europe in the year 1348 and in the course of two years is thought to have reduced the population by between one-third and one-half.

It is when we think of the Black Death and its consequences that we are able to appreciate most strongly the helplessness of mediaeval people in the face of infectious disease. Plague is of two kinds, which are known as pneumonic and bubonic plague. The former, which attacks the lungs, is spread by the breath, while the latter is accompanied by painful swellings, or buboes, in the groin and beneath the armpits. The medical men of the day were not fools and they did their best: in fact one of their number, Guy de Chauliac, was able to deduce the difference between the two types. What they failed to discover, however, was that bubonic plague was spread by the bite of the flea which initially lived off the body of the plague rat, which meant that the doctors were tragically ignorant of the fact that the problem was largely one of sanitation. For, both in town and village, the plague rat lived freely off the stinking filth that was left rotting in the streets. Mediaeval towns and villages may have been romantically beautiful: but they were reeking death traps nevertheless.

It is hardly surprising, in view of what has been said, that mediaeval people should have shown themselves to have been obsessed with the idea of death, or that they should consistently have thought of death as a horrid skeletal figure who stalked from place to place, striking down men and women suddenly and without discrimination between rich and poor. Death was the great equalizer whom no man could escape (Plate 8, between pages 64 and 65, *Death and the Cardinal*). In considering the

15

strength of this obsession we need to bear in mind the sharp effect of the 'invisible striker' upon an exceedingly thin population. For the population of Europe was minute when compared with that of modern times. The whole population of England could have been comfortably housed in half the sprawl of modern London. We should not, however, be misled into thinking that the stresses of mediaeval life resulted in a people permanently bowed down with misery and depression. As we shall see, the contrary is true. History teaches us that stresses of the sort with which we are dealing here usually serve to increase the human appetite for living.

There are still two details of Latimer's description which call for comment. The first of these is the fact that Latimer's father kept him at school. This would have been comparatively rare even in Latimer's day, though the importance of literacy was certainly beginning to receive greater emphasis as the mediaeval period drew to its close. Literacy had been regarded very much as the prerogative of churchmen, though even among the poorer parish clergy there were some who could do little more than stagger through the Latin of the divine office, parrot fashion. Hugh Latimer who, of course, was far from illiterate, rose to be Bishop of Worcester.

Finally, there is the reference to godliness: and here it will be necessary to speak in far more general terms, for by 'godliness' a number of things could have been meant. Doubtless, Latimer's father would have paid his tithe (one-tenth of his produce) with regularity to the Church, and possibly with less reluctance than most. He would have attended his parish church faithfully, at least on every festival day. As for his belief in God, this would not necessarily have made him puritanical in his opinions or in his morals (strict morality, it seems, was never an outstanding feature of mediaeval life). It would, however, have provided, as it did for the majority of mediaeval people, the sole anchorage for his mind in the course of a life which was bristling with danger, and terrifyingly unpredictable.

Here we must leave Latimer and his father to add a brief and final introductory note concerning the Christian culture from which the mediaeval theatre sprang.

The period covered by this book extends from the tenth century to the end of the fifteenth century. This means that we take up our theme at a time when the gradual Christianization of the savage peoples whose migrations and invasions had coincided with the collapse of the Roman Empire, had already been in progress for more than three hundred years. But, for reasons which do not concern us in this book, the process was far from complete by the tenth century so that the congregations of people who took part in the Christian ritual of the Mass were still almost entirely illiterate and barely civilized. This is a point of considerable importance to us here. For the mediaeval stage in Europe began as an educative medium through which the Church illustrated to the unlearned the significance of its festivals and the legends around which the whole body of the Christian faith had developed. We shall see how these early dramatic illustrations evolved within the church building itself, ultimately to become a great outdoor theatre in their own right, popular in the truest sense of the word.

But a theatre is expressive, not merely of the art of the performer, but of the heart and soul of its audience as well. It is in our understanding of the latter that we need to approach the subject with complete detachment and independence of mind, undisturbed by our modern conception of things. If we are able to do that, then the mediaeval theatre audience will appear before us, not as sharply outlined as we should wish, of course, for that would not be possible; but at least sufficiently to reveal something of its zest, its love of colourful festival, its sense of pathos, and its robust sense of irreverent comedy. The one thing above all we must not expect is an expression of the Christian faith which is merely pious and moralistic. To these people, Christianity was a vivid interpretation of the deepest terrors and highest hopes of which they were capable. Nor was the interpretation wholly Christian in the modern sense, since much of it was, to the very end of the period, more than a little charged with the pagan superstitions of pre-Christian times. We have only to look round mediaeval church buildings to find sufficient evidence of this. The drawing shown in Figure 1, for example, which is taken from the fifteenth-century main doorway at Iver Church in Buckinghamshire, is frankly pagan in origin. What we see is a head carved in stone, wearing a crown and having an oak leaf protruding from its mouth. We get the impression of an ugly, sinister little fellow; and he becomes even more sinister when we learn something of his history. For he is the Green Man, or Jack-in-the-Green as he is sometimes called.

17

Fig. 1　The foliate head of the Green Man, carved in stone at Iver Church, Buckinghamshire

Before Christianity came along to tame him, he was a fertility god whose rites included the burning alive of human beings and animals in a cage made from the boughs of bushes and trees. Many mediaeval customs, such as the morris and maypole dances, are indicative of the undercurrent of pagan sentiment that remained in the popular mediaeval mind. Nor is this to be wondered at when it is considered how closely familiar the people were with the mystery of the earth, the significance of the rising sun and the life-giving properties of the rain in season. It is a sign of the wisdom of the Church that its major festivals should have followed so closely the rhythm of the solar year.

As a final indication of the need for an open mind in assessing the impact of mediaeval drama upon the audience of its time, we might anticipate a little and consider an example from one of the better-known Miracle plays which was performed when the mediaeval theatre was at the highest point of its popularity. It comes from the Chester play of the *Deluge* where God is portrayed in an angry mood and is about to destroy the whole world because his favourite creation, Man, has persistently disobeyed him:

> Man that I made I will destroy,
> 　Beast, worm, and fowl to fly,
> For on earth they me annoy*　　　　　[*injure grievously]
> 　The folk that is thereon.

How do we interpret this stage figure of God: and how do we assess its probable impact upon the audience of its time? Is it the

18

one true God of the Christian faith? Is it perhaps a single aspect of him? Is it possibly the image of an angry, revenging nature god conjured up from the tribal past and coloured by Christian legend? Or is it simply the caricature of an angry, destructive old man? Perhaps there is an element of truth suggested by each of these questions. But as soon as we take into consideration that the dramatic image was conceived during the fourteenth century in the course of which two shattering disasters occurred, this figure of God becomes not merely credible, but a figure of terrifying authority. The first disaster consisted of torrential rains, which in the years 1314/15 destroyed the crops so utterly that many thousands of people died of famine. The second was the Black Death of 1348/49, which has already been mentioned.

It is by thus trying to view the ritual and drama of the mediaeval theatre in the light of the contemporary human background that the serious student can extract the maximum satisfaction from his subject. For there are two major characteristics of the mediaeval theatre which need to be constantly borne in mind. In the first place, it was a theatre rooted in Christian legend and therefore focused to a considerable extent upon events of the past. Secondly, because it was the natural habit of mediaeval play-wrights to think in terms of contemporary experience they produced a theatre which was essentially of their own time. Both of these characteristics need to be explained in some detail, and I shall, of course, be referring to them in the present book from time to time.

2

THE THEATRE OF
THE EARLY CHURCH

The sketch in Figure 2a shows the ground plan of a typical English church of the eleventh century: the kind of church, in other words, that was built by the Anglo-Saxons before the Norman Conquest, and by the Normans themselves for many years after that event. You can see that the building is divided into two parts, namely, part A, which has a semi-circular wall or apse at its end and is known as the Sanctuary, and the rectangular part B, which we call the Nave or the place occupied by the congregation. Separating the two parts is an arch C.

If you turn now to the Plates section you will see photographs showing what the interiors of these early churches looked like. Plates 2A and 2B show the sanctuary and nave of the Saxon church at Worth, Sussex, while Plate 2C shows the inside of the Norman church at Kilpeck in Herefordshire. Both churches remain very much as they were when their Saxon and Norman builders completed them. Note, by the way, that the church at Kilpeck has a feature which is lacking in the Saxon church. It has two arches instead of one, the space in between being known as the Chancel, or singing place. The chancel is of special importance to us because it played a vital part in the ritual and the drama of the mediaeval Church. Figure 2b shows a ground plan of a church of this type.

Now, it would not be difficult for anyone who is familiar with the modern theatre to recognize in the photograph of Kilpeck Church certain interesting points of comparison with the interior of a theatre building of the proscenium type: in fact, so close are these points of comparison that it is possible, simply by altering the names given to the various parts, to make the two types of building completely interchangeable. Thus, for *sanctuary* we can read

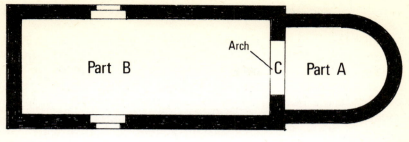

2a

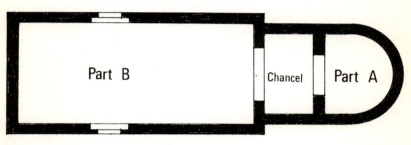

2b

Fig. 2a   A simple two-cell church

Fig. 2b   A three-cell church with a chancel

Note   See also Plates 2A, 2B and 2C.

stage; for *sanctuary arch* we can read *proscenium arch*; instead of the *chancel* we have the *stage apron* or that part of the stage floor which projects beyond the proscenium arch. Finally, and quite obviously, for *nave* we can read *auditorium*, though we have to remember that the nave of the mediaeval church building contained no seats or pews.

These similarities are not merely accidental or imaginary. The mediaeval church building was a theatre in the truest sense of the word, namely, a place in which an act or performance by one or more persons can be witnessed or 'shared' by an audience or congregation. It was designed, therefore, strictly in accordance with its function, with a stage upon which the performance could take place and an area set apart for those who witnessed and shared in it.

If we are to understand the drama of the Middle Ages it will be necessary to learn as much as we can about the theatrical purpose of the building in which it took root and developed into a conscious art. This is a process of study which it is better not to confine to the reading of books. There are still churches to be found in the British Isles which, like Kilpeck, remain just as their Saxon or Norman builders designed them, and there are many others which, although they have been enlarged and embellished in the course of time, still reveal traces of their original fabric. To be able to plot from such evidences the plan of a mediaeval church as it was first built is an interesting skill which may be acquired with practice, and the research involved carries with it the additional reward of bringing us into more intimate contact with the folk for whom the theatre of the church represented a complete way of life. There are still many ancient churches to be found in which mediaeval wall paintings and painted glass windows have survived to help us to interpret the inspiration lying behind the mediaeval dramatic theme, while the works of many craftsmen in stone and wood remain to inform us of the zest for living, the sense of humour and farcical irreverence, as well as the horror of death and bodily corruption, which beset the consciousness of a mediaeval theatre audience. All these evidences are there for the seeking and, no matter whether the search is conducted alone, or in a party with the help of an informed guide, or whether it takes place in a great cathedral church like Canterbury, Peterborough or Durham, or in a tiny parish church like Kilpeck, it will always be found interesting, and sometimes great fun too.

Now, I have already pointed out in the introductory chapter that the mediaeval play evolved from the Christian ritual of the Mass, a ritual which itself contained a number of important dramatic elements. Since the primary function of the mediaeval church building lay in the performance of this ritual, we shall now briefly consider it, bearing in mind that the most important elements of the drama as we understand it consist, first, of the sense of conflict, and then of the communicative arts of dialogue, whether sung or spoken, and of movement in combination with mime. As we shall see, the mediaeval church building, especially when it was equipped with a chancel, was admirably suited to the performance of the ritual, particularly if we remember that ritual, like the play, is a shared experience between performer and audience.

The celebration of the Mass involves a sacred mystery and the performance of a sacrifice. It still represents the most important act of worship among millions of Roman Catholics in the world today and, with certain important variations in name and inter-pretation, of members of other Christian denominations as well. In the modern world, however, the approach of civilized peoples to what we should now describe as religious matters is so sharply in contrast with what the approach of the average mediaeval Christian would have been, that much confusion is likely to arise if we fail to take note of some of the differences.

To us, religious belief, or rather belief in God, is a matter of personal choice. Our act of choosing may be the result of deeply reasoned thought, or it may be sparked off by a sudden rush of inspiration or perhaps of conscience. It may even be the result of prejudice. But whichever way it is, we always regard the choice as a personal one, and we should certainly consider it rude and intrusive to expect our neighbours, or even our closest friends and relatives, to make the same choice as we do. This is an approach to the matter which an average person living in, say, the twelfth or the thirteenth century, would have found puzzling, to say the least. This is because the question of choice would never have arisen for such a person in the first place. To have questioned the existence of God would have been like questioning the greenness of grass or the wetness of water. All were equally obvious, and to have questioned them or to have formed opinions about them would have been stupid.

What lay behind the unquestioning belief of mediaeval people in the existence of God was their simple sense of the miraculous. To them all life was plainly a miracle. They were alive, and because only divine power could perform and sustain miracles they believed in God. It was as simple as that.

We usually sum up the contrast between the two ways of think-ing by saying that our approach to life and religion is critical, rationalistic and scientific while that of the mediaeval mind was acceptive. This does not mean that mediaeval people were in-capable of scepticism or doubt: it simply means that they accepted with the certainty of truth many things which we

23

automatically submit to the test of doubt. The difference is exceedingly important to us in this book, and particularly so when we come to consider the theatrical effect of Christian ritual. We have to think all the time of an audience which would never have felt at home with our ways of thinking about God. With this in mind let us now turn our attention to the Mass and the beliefs with which it was concerned.

The sacrificial ritual of the Mass perpetuated within the mediaeval mind what all Christians believe to be the two major processes governing the life of mankind. Stated in terms of religious doctrine the processes are as follows:

Man originally existed in a state of innocence. He knew no evil and was immortal. Through temptation and pride he learned of the existence of evil and in doing so fell from his state of innocence and received the burdens of conflict, labour and mortality. But God took pity upon Man in his guilt and sent his son into the world to become a human sacrifice in the name of Divine Love, the only agent through which Man might be restored to his original state, free from evil and pride. The name of this son was Jesus, the Christ or Messiah who was born in Bethlehem during the time when the Romans governed the Jews. Jesus, when he was grown to manhood, went about preaching a new law of love of God and love of one's neighbour in defiance of the Hebrew priests and lawyers who opposed him. In the course of his mission Jesus miraculously healed many sick people in the name of the Divine Love represented by his Father, but his Jewish enemies, jealous for the old moral law, denounced him before the Roman governor and he was put to death by crucifixion, a disgraceful and agonizing form of death reserved for the lowest criminals. Jesus was buried in a sepulchre but after three days he rose and appeared again among his disciples. Thus, through the physical sacrifice of Jesus, the Son of God, Man was introduced to the second of the two processes: that of redemption from evil and the promise of ultimate restoration to his original state of innocence.

In purely theatrical terms the two processes may be seen as those of tragedy (Man's disastrous fall from the state of innocence) and romantic, or in this case, divine, comedy (Man's uplifting through the sufferings of Jesus and his ultimate redemption thereby). The theatrical connection is very important, as we shall see.

Now, the ritual of the Mass seeks to satisfy its religious purpose in two ways, the first of which is historical and commemorative. In the Gospel of St Matthew, Chapter 26, we read how Jesus partook of the Feast of the Passover in the company of his disciples on the night before he died. In full prophetic consciousness of the fate that awaited him, Jesus broke bread and distributed wine in a most significant way which is told in the following words:

And as they were eating, Jesus took bread, and blessed it, and brake it, and gave it to the disciples, and said, Take, eat; this is my body.

And he took the cup, and gave thanks, and gave it to them, saying, Drink ye all of it.

For this is my blood of the new testament which is shed for many for the remission of sins.

In the course of the Mass, bread is eaten and wine drunk as was done at the Last Supper. Regarded in the light of drama, it can be seen as an act of pure humility in the face of an appalling human tragedy in which innocence was to be tortured, humiliated and ultimately slaughtered to satisfy the lowest passions of men.

But the second object of the Mass is to perform a mystery or miracle. This is the mystery of the transubstantiation in which the bread and wine are changed into the body and blood of the crucified Jesus, so that those who take part in the ritual are able to become 'one' with their God. This is the miraculous change which requires the offices of a priest, as we shall see.

The ordering, or what we call the 'liturgy', of the Mass has changed very little during the past thousand years. Nevertheless, in view of the differences, some of which have already been mentioned, that existed between the mediaeval view of things and our own, we should expect the dramatic impact of the ritual also to be different. We shall consider briefly, but in a certain amount of detail, the way in which the Mass was and is conducted. But in order that we can try as much as possible to see the ritual through mediaeval eyes, we shall need to expand a little more upon some of the characteristics of the mediaeval mind.

I have already pointed out the 'acceptiveness' of mediaeval people in their belief in God. But this was just as much a characteristic of their belief in other things, particularly when those things were incapable of being seen, or were, as we say, abstract. Now, hand in hand with this 'acceptiveness' there went an exceedingly vivid sense of imagery which they employed to give life and shape to their ideas. Thus, for them the concepts of good and evil were represented by living, supernatural shapes: on the one hand, ugly, terrifying creatures, half-human, half-animal, belonging to the fiery nether-world of Satan, and on the other, celestial figures of angels, the gloriously winged companions of God. These were the embattled hosts sprung from the original war in Heaven when God's favourite angel, Lucifer, Son of the Morning, rebelled in his pride against his Lord and was expelled from Heaven to become Satan, the Prince of Darkness and Lord of Hell, the leader of the fallen angels, now transformed into devils, who had rebelled with him. And here we come to the conflict which was fundamental to all mediaeval Christians. They accepted without question all that a modern agnostic, and many a modern Christian too, would regard as poetic legend. To them the conflict between the powers of light and darkness was real, personal, and of everyday familiarity: a life and death struggle of vividly imagined supernatural beings with the possession of every man's soul as its ultimate purpose. This was the universal conflict or 'stress' which inspired the whole of the mediaeval drama. We need to bear it in mind when we attempt to assess the impact on mediaeval people of the ritual of the Mass, which I shall now briefly describe.

The degree of ceremony which accompanied the ritual might vary considerably. It might be a simple affair calling for the presence of only one priest, or it might be sufficiently elaborate to require a number of assistants for the priest and in addition, a choir or chorus. We shall consider a celebration of the more elaborate kind, so that we have to imagine a priest, together with his assistants, performing their parts in the sanctuary; a choir of men and boys occupying the chancel; and the congregation who remain in the nave.

The ceremony begins with a solemn procession of priests and choristers who enter the church in the presence of the congregation. The impression given is of colourful theatricality with the priests wearing the embroidered robes of their sacred office, and the choir clad in their choir robes.

As soon as the chancel is filled the first part of the ritual begins. This is an act of purification to prepare those present for the sacrifice in which they are to share. The preparation consists of prayer, most of which is intoned or sung; songs of praise and supplication; the singing of certain of the Psalms of David; the reading by one of the priests of passages from the Gospels; the declaration by the chorus, representing the whole assembly, of the articles of the Christian faith (the Creed); and an offering of gifts for the poor.

An observer, present at the ceremony for the first time, would be struck by the fact that the whole proceeding is conducted in the Latin tongue. In mediaeval times Latin was the universal language of the Western Church: in fact, it was regarded as the universal language of all literate Europeans during the period. Only sermons, when they were delivered, were spoken in the native tongue. This will be a useful point to remember later on.

The next thing that claims our attention is the way in which many of the prayers and songs get their shape and emphasis from what appears to be a carefully devised system of responses. Sometimes a priest will intone a line or a verse and the choir, or perhaps the choir and congregation together, will reply. One simple example is frequently heard as an introduction to prayers:

Priest
Dominus vobiscum   [The Lord be with you]

Chorus and/or Congregation
Et cum spiritu tuo   [And with thy spirit]

Priest
Oremus   [Let us pray]

This is dialogue which is given *form* and nearly approaches art because, being a part of ritual, it occurs in deliberately arranged places. When the same method is applied to an anthem calling upon the people to glorify God the effect is exciting: bordering very closely upon the dramatic:

Priest
Gloria in excelsis Deo   [Glory to God in the highest]

Chorus
Et in terra pax hominibus   [And on earth peace,
bonae voluntatis.   goodwill towards men.
Laudamus te.   We praise thee,
Benedicimus te.   we bless thee,
Adoramus te.   we adore thee,
Glorificamus te ——   we glorify thee ——]

27

If you are a student of Greek as well as mediaeval drama you will have little difficulty in comparing the function of the priest here with that of the chorus leader in early Greek tragedy. In both cases the 'leader' draws out a response from the chorus which in turn becomes the representative of the people as a whole. This is the dramatic essence of all popular ritual.

There is yet another parallel to be found with the Greek theatre in the singing or chanting of alternate verses by parts or sections of the chorus. This division of a choir into semi-choruses, which we call antiphonal singing, tends to impart to the verses the dramatic effect of statement and counter-statement. In the case of the Greek chorus, however, additional dramatic emphasis was given by the dancing which accompanied the choral singing.

The apparent absence of dancing from the Christian ritual calls for comment. From the earliest days of the Christian faith dancing was suppressed because of its pagan associations. Yet if we look carefully at the behaviour of the priests in their performance of the Mass we shall see that dancing of a sort does in fact take place. At given points throughout the ceremony the priests change their positions in the sanctuary. Sometimes they face the congregation and at others they turn and face the altar. In addition to this they are frequently seen to bow and, as we say, genuflect (bend the knee) before the altar. All these movements are solemn and deliberate. They are also symbolic; and because they occur at stated times according to the demands of the ritual they form a pattern of movement that is not far removed from that of a ritual dance. Moreover, the movements themselves, because they are formal and exaggerated, bear a strong resemblance to theatrical miming, as anyone who has practised the art of mime will readily understand.

So far we have spoken of the priests in their function as leaders of chorus and audience or congregation. When we come to the second part of the Mass we see them standing out more clearly in their true character of priests because it is here that the sacred mystery is performed over which they, and they alone, can preside. All eyes become focused upon one priest in particular who takes position immediately in front of the altar. He is the 'celebrant' under whose hands and by whose prayers the miraculous change will take place which will render the bread and wine into the flesh and blood of the crucified Christ. The solemnity of what he is about to do is expressed by the chorus in their singing of the *Sanctus*:

Chorus	
Sanctus,	[Holy,
sanctus,	holy,
sanctus,	holy,
Dominus, Deus Sabaoth,	Lord God of hosts,
Pleni sunt coeli et terra	heaven and earth are full
gloria tua ———	of your glory ———]

Some of the prayers offered by the celebrant are 'secret'; that is to say, they are heard by him alone. Others are spoken aloud for the benefit of all people present. All are reminded of the sacrificial act of redemption from sin when God in the Flesh, in the person of Jesus, suffered death, only to triumph over death in becoming restored to life. Due emphasis to this, the most solemn moment in Christian experience, is given by the celebrant in a number of symbolic gestures, of which one is the stretching out of his arms as though in the agony of crucifixion. But the essential

Fig. 3   The mimetic crucifixion gesture of a priest celebrating Mass

climax of the drama is reached at the point of 'consecration' when the bread becomes the Host or body of the crucified Jesus. The celebrant immediately elevates the Host above his head and a bell is rung.

Now, at this point of climax we see the celebrant priest performing very much as an actor performs. How far his words and gestures are intended as a direct impersonation of the crucified Jesus and how far they are merely symbolical must depend mainly upon the priest's personal reaction to his task. Whatever he does, however, his performance must represent a verbal, visual and emotional experience which he shares with his audience or congregation. To that extent he becomes an actor.

Following upon the consecration there comes the Kiss of Peace which introduces the solemn act of Communion. The Kiss of Peace, which commemorates the words of Jesus to his disciples, 'Peace I leave with you, my peace I give unto you,' is passed from the celebrant to the first of his assistant priests who passes it on to the next assistant. Thus the grave symbolical act is passed from priests to choir, and so on. All is now ready for the Communion of the people who advance and fall on their knees to receive the consecrated Host from the hands of the celebrant and his assistant priests.

Now, if we sum up the elements of drama and theatre which appear from our brief glimpse of the Roman Mass, we get the following list:

1   Tragedy   the presentation of the sufferings and death of Jesus the Christ.

2   Divine Comedy   the resurrection of Jesus and, through his sacrifice, the redemption of mankind.

3   Catharsis   the sense of release or purging from sin (see also below).

4   Dialogue   through verse and response, and the division of the choir into semi-choruses.

5   Miming   in the gestures of the celebrant and the suggestion of dance in the ceremonial movements of the priests.

But what, it may well be asked, of *Chance* which we have already seen as a vital element in all communal ritual? The answer to this question is implicit in item 3 on our list. In plain practical terms, it is the main purpose of the Christian ritual to release the faithful from the stress of the conflict between the powers of good and evil. Hence the use of the word *Catharsis* which, when employed in a theatrical sense, simply means release from stress or emotion. As we shall see in a later chapter, to mediaeval people the moral conflict of earthly experience was acutely important, and the consequences of defeat, that is of failure to gain redemption from sin, were dreadful in the extreme. These were the 'chances' involved in the Mass, and the more we get to understand the minds and the point of view of these people, the more readily shall we appreciate the urgency of their religious question, 'What will happen to *Us*?'

Ritual, however, although it is essentially theatrical, and although it contains the elements of drama, does not constitute a play, for a play requires a number of special components which are not to be found in ritual. It must have a plot or 'legend', and it must involve the impersonation of a character by an actor. Above all, it must draw the attention of its audience towards the affairs of people other than themselves so that the crucial question becomes, not so much, 'What will happen to *Us*?' as 'What will happen to *Them*?'

This change in audience attention or interest is a gradual one, and it usually begins with a need to demonstrate and, through demonstration, to explain, certain happenings. This was certainly the case with the early Greek drama, and it was the case with mediaeval drama as well.

We have already seen that the Mass, including the gospel readings, was conducted in the Latin tongue. This means that there must have been a serious language gap between those who performed the ritual and their audience, or at least a large part of it, for most of the spectators would have been illiterate in any case. But the gospels were to the Christian what the ancient Greek legends were to the worshippers of the pagan nature gods. They represented the historical basis of the ritual. In other words, without an understanding of the legend the ritual became a nonsense. Here was something which required demonstration and we shall now deal with the way in which the play evolved as a means to satisfy this need.

31

3

THE GROWTH OF
THE DRAMATIC IDEA

We have already seen how, during his performance of the Mass, the officiating priest undertakes the functions of a chorus leader, and how at a given point in the ceremony the part played by him closely approaches that of an actor. Let us now examine an altogether different kind of ceremony which began at a very early date in the history of the Christian Church. This was the ritual associated with the consecration of a new church building which had to take place before any sacred office could be permitted within its walls. Basically the purpose of the ritual was the cleansing of the building from any spirit of evil which might lurk within, and it was a ritual which had to be performed by the Bishop.

The ceremony began with the Bishop, attended by other members of the clergy and a choir, approaching the main door of the building and rapping upon it with his staff, at the same time uttering the following words of command which are taken from Psalm 24:

Tollite portas!   [Lift up your heads, O ye gates!]

Now, there are two verses of Psalm 24 which played, as, indeed, they continue to play, a very important part in the rite of church consecration. Doubtless the verses were originally sung by the choir, or perhaps uttered by the Bishop alone. By the ninth century, however, they had become so adapted that they offered a short passage of dramatic dialogue plus a little piece of symbolic miming which presented to the onlookers something resembling a very short play. Let us first look at the two verses so that we can see precisely in what manner they were adapted. Here they are in the English translation of the Book of Common Prayer:

Lift up your heads O ye gates, and be ye lift up ye everlasting doors: and the King of glory shall come in.
Who is the King of glory: even the Lord of hosts, he is the King of glory.

The adaptation that we have comes from the city of Metz in French Lorraine and it was recorded during the ninth century. It directs that before the approach of the Bishop and his retinue a member of the clergy shall enter the building and remain hidden behind the main door. The following episode then takes place:

The Bishop on reaching the closed door raps upon it three times with his staff, and at the same time declaims the first verse:

'Lift up your heads O ye gates and be ye lift up ye everlasting doors: and the King of glory shall come in.'

The member of the clergy hidden within then cries out the challenging question:

'Who is the King of glory?'

Then comes the general cry:

'Even the Lord of hosts, he is the King of glory.'

Upon which the hidden man flings open the doors and comes running wildly out, ultimately to join the procession at the rear while the Bishop makes his entry to claim the building in the name of God.

Now, here we get a very early example of mimed symbolism in which the hidden person acts the part of the spirit of evil cast out by the Bishop. It is an episode, of course, which might easily be dismissed by a modern cynic as a piece of mumbo-jumbo intended to impress an illiterate populace. But such an interpretation by seizing upon a half-truth would miss all the aspects of the whole truth, and in so doing would fail to grasp at least two important points of theatrical linkage between an audience of the ninth century and an audience of our own time. The first point is related to the impact of mimed symbolism itself which I shall try to explain by citing a highly popular modern example, namely, that of the bearer of the Olympic torch at the commencement of the Olympic games.

Whether we as individuals are interested in athletic pursuits or not, we are always ready to accept on a world-wide scale the festival spirit of the Olympic games, no matter in what country they are celebrated, though we may or may not know that the festival, together with its ideals, originally evolved in ancient

Greece and in honour of the god Zeus. The carrying of the Olympic flame by relays of runners across the continents of the world to the appointed Olympic stadium is watched with universal interest and reported from day to day in our newspapers and on radio and television. The entry of the last runner into the stadium and the lighting of the Olympic fire from the flame of the torch in the presence of the competitors and of a vast public audience is a dramatic moment which, in its symbolism, perpetuates a human ideal which is underlined by the declaration of the Olympic oath by one or two of the competitors, representing the whole company. As for the torch-bearer himself, he is all-important when he enters the stadium, though he fades into insignificance as soon as his function is performed. The reason is simple. He begins as a part of a symbol—a theatrically demonstrative figure who in the universal language of physical action makes clear to the many what may be expressed in terms of language only by the few. As soon as he relinquishes the Olympic flame he becomes an ordinary person.

Our second linkage point is possibly even more significant than the first. The use of the priest in the mediaeval ceremony to symbolize the spirit of evil hidden within the new building may strike us as crude when we consider it as a piece of stage contrivance—as little more than a charade, in fact. Whatever impact it had upon its ninth-century audience must have depended, therefore, upon the liveliness of their own imaginations and upon their own interpretation of evil as a spirit or quality in human experience. It is, of course, impossible to say exactly how the episode was received, but we do know something of the way in which mediaeval people, very much like the pagans before them, associated evil with all death-dealing and life-opposing spirits, and with what horror they visualized such spirits in their imaginations. It was the business of the Church, particularly in those early days of our civilization, to guide the imaginations of people towards the purer, less earthly and more permanent values of the Christian faith: and the living, theatrically 'demonstrative' figure of the hidden priest and his wild escape from the presence of the Bishop was obviously introduced with that object in view. Evil, as symbolized by the priest who runs wildly like a devil, is confronted by Good as symbolized by the Bishop who is God's representative. The conflict between the two is inevitable, and evil is the loser. And here we get our point of linkage.

The conflict between the powers of good and evil has been a consistently productive source of popular entertainment from the ninth century to the present day. We still have our conflicts between 'goodies' and 'baddies' on the stage and on cinema and television screens, no matter whether they appear in popular 'Westerns' or against the futuristic background of science fiction. Now, because theatrical entertainment depends to a very large extent upon the degree of 'illusion' that takes place in ourselves as members of the audience, it follows that the more absorbed we become in the entertainment, the more whole-heartedly we believe in the characters who are engaged in the conflict— at least, for as long as the play or film lasts. But these characters are no more real in a human sense than are the figures of the priest and the Bishop. Their behaviour, no matter whether they are 'goodies' or 'baddies', is wholly predictable, and so is the outcome of the conflict. When they convince us, it is simply in order to satisfy our wish to see the bad overcome by the good, for which reason they are living symbols rather than complete human beings, more cunningly contrived perhaps than the simple mediaeval episode, but nevertheless indicative of the fact that our basic sense of values has changed very little during the past thousand years.

But the consecration ceremony, whatever its importance to us as a dramatized incident, was not a complete dramatic idea. For although the Bishop and the hidden priest provided symbols of conflict, neither of them represented 'characters' in a dramatic sense. For this to take place some sort of story, plot or legend had to be introduced, and for the addition of this ingredient we have to look to the major festivals of the Church.

When a religious ritual evolves into a drama it usually does so in order to communicate a mystic legend concerning the life of the god in whose name the ritual is celebrated. This seems to have been the case with the drama of the ancient Greeks. It was certainly the case with the mediaeval Christian theatre.

Our main business in the present chapter lies with the festivals of Christmas and Easter. And here again we have to try to imagine something of the impact of Christian ceremony during the remote period of the ninth and tenth centuries upon people whose reactions to the elements and to the seasonal changes of the year were never far removed from the reactions of pagans. The festival of Christmas fell in mid-winter which, for people living in the northern hemisphere, was around the shortest day in the year. It was a season of intense cold, scarcity of food and general hardship when people looked forward with great longing to the return of the sun and the heart-warming promise of the miraculous renewal of the yearly cycle. Easter was a festival of the spring when the hopes of men and women centred upon the fertility of the soil and the upsurge of new growth. For countless generations people had at this exciting time of the year danced and sung in honour of their tribal fertility gods and goddesses. The very name of the Easter festival, it is worth remembering, had been derived from the name of the month devoted to the worship of Eostre the earth goddess.

It was characteristic of the Christian festivals that they should have followed the seasonal rhythm of the year very much in the manner of the pagan festivals with their worship of nature gods. The result was that each festival was able to make a double impact upon the people, the one essentially Christian and the other earthily pagan in sentiment. Thus, the worship of the infant Jesus and the commemoration of his birth at Christmas was able to go hand in hand with the eager anticipation of the birth of a new year with all its hopes and its fears. Still closer, perhaps, was the parallel offered by Easter with its story of the death and restoration to life of a man who was to the true Christian, God in the flesh. Here was the story of a god restored to life which must have challenged the imaginations of those whose habitual thoughts in the spring of the year lay with the revival of the life-giving earth spirit. In one sense the God of Christianity was struggling against the pagan gods and images of the all-too-recent past. If he was to conquer, and in so doing found a new civilization, it could only be by supplanting the images and legends of the pagan world with those of Christianity. Were the problem one of our own day, we should no doubt decide that the best means to a solution lay with the wise use of 'communications media'. This was precisely the way in which the Christian Church looked at the matter and it was from two such media, namely those of symbol and song, that the art of mediaeval drama sprang.

The most complete picture available to us of early dramatic

development evolves around Easter, the most important of all the Christian festivals, and, as we might expect, the symbol employed was that of the cross. The theatre of every church carried its cross, or rood as it was called in mediaeval times. This usually occupied a dominant position high above the chancel or choir, frequently on a beam known as the rood beam. The student who undertakes a thorough study of the theatre of the mediaeval church will be bound at some time to come across a stairway which once gave access to such a beam—it may now apparently lead nowhere except to a cavity cut high in the chancel arch with a clear drop beyond. Plate 3 shows a stairway of this description at Iver in Buckinghamshire. The chief interest of such a stairway lies in the use to which it was put during the festival of Easter. For on Good Friday, the day of the execution of Jesus, the cross was taken down and reverently removed, either to the north side of the altar where it was covered with a white cloth, or to a place known as the Easter Sepulchre (either a niche or an existing tomb set in the north wall of the sanctuary, or a structure specially built for the purpose). Men were set to watch over the veiled cross, as though keeping vigil over a dead body, until the morning of Easter Sunday, when the cross was unveiled and restored to its former position, always with reverence and in some churches with impressive ceremony.

The significance of this symbolic 'deposition' and 'elevation' of the cross lay, of course, in the association of the crucifix with the body of Christ: its entombment and ultimate resurrection. Herein lay the mystery and triumph of the Christian faith with its promise of eternal life, salvation, love and mercy for mankind: and it was naturally fitting that the legend associated with the mystery should be demonstrated, and in due course acted, in order to 'fortify' the faith of the illiterate and uninformed. The play, which is known to students of mediaeval drama by the opening words of its dialogue *Quem quaeritis* ('Whom do you seek?'), developed from a form of singing called trope singing. This was a form of chanting from which many dramatic ideas of the early Christian world were to grow, so it might be helpful to pause while something is said about it by way of explanation.

Trope singing, because of its highly elaborate nature, usually suggests to us a rather over-developed or long-winded form of Christian ceremonial. It sprang, nevertheless, from the simple and perfectly natural impulse in people to emphasize in terms of song their reaction to the works or acts of God—and here it must be remembered that to the Christian, God and Christ are in a very subtle sense one. Those of us to whom 'trope' is a strange word may begin to understand something of its meaning, together with the sort of impulse that lies behind it, by trying to imagine a modern example of what may be described as a trope in a very raw and unformed state. We ought to be able to do this if we return once more to the football chorus to which we referred in the first chapter, far cry though the football ground is from the theatre of the church.

Most football 'fans' single out a player from their side who becomes the object of their special affection and pride. Such a player will have proved his skill by his deeds as a striker, a defender, or perhaps as a master-tactician, with the result that his name is on every supporter's lips, and, most particularly, on those of the massed 'football chorus' who will chant it whenever they feel the need to encourage the player to the point of maximum, or even superhuman, effort. Let us imagine such a player and let us suppose that his name is John Smith, in which case he will most likely be known to all and sundry as Johnny. We shall also suppose him to be a striker.

Now, as soon as Johnny enters into the drama of a game of football, either by threatening to score a goal or by actually doing so, his name will most likely be taken up by the supporting 'football chorus' and rendered in a way that has become familiar to anyone who has an acquaintance with league football. The name is chanted in what in musical terms is called a 'falling phrase' of two notes, each of which is sufficiently prolonged to express affection bordering upon adoration: 'Johnnn-ieeee!'

The chanting of Johnny's name in this way does not in itself comprise a trope. It does, however, represent a verbal and musical elaboration of a name or word and helps us to understand similar elaborations which began to develop during the early years of the Christian Church. One of the commonest words to become so elaborated during this period was *alleluia*, which literally means, 'Praise ye Jehovah' [God]. If we are able to develop our football example into a trope, we shall have to use our imaginations a little further and put into words the thoughts which *might* be passing through the minds of the 'football chorus' at the time of their chanting. If during an exciting point of attack it appeared that Johnny was about to score a goal, a very likely thought or wish would be 'Johnny, score a goal now!' This would simply amount to a bald statement of will or encouragement and would still not constitute a trope. If, however, the statement were extended to include *either* an appreciation of the player's skill *or* a reference to an event in the past which was indicative of that skill, then it would offer us a crude example of a trope. Here are some imaginary examples:

Trope A
Johnny, *the most skilful of strikers*, score a goal now!

Trope B
Johnny, *who brilliantly scored the winning goal against X Town last week*, score a goal now!

It is important to note that in either case it is only the part of the sentence printed in italics that really constitutes the trope which, of course, would have to be sung.

Now, Trope B relates an event, and we can easily extend our analogy a little further to show how it might be projected into a play, either short or long. The simple demonstration in terms of action of the goal scored by Johnny last week would give us an exceedingly short play. If, however, the action were to include a series of events in the life of Johnny showing how he became a football hero, then the play might run to a considerable length. What we are concerned with at the present time is a development of a not dissimilar nature, though it is related to the chief events of Christian legend.

The trope which formed the basis of the Easter play was a repetition of the account given in the New Testament of the resurrection of Jesus on the third day after his execution, and its discovery by the three women who went to visit his tomb. To their amazement they found the great stone which had sealed the entrance to the tomb rolled away. On entering they encountered an angel, in the form of a young man 'clothed in a white garment', who told them that Jesus was no longer in the tomb but had risen from the dead. He urged the women not to fear but to depart and spread the marvellous news. The simplest trope known to us which is founded upon this theme comes from St Gall in Switzerland. Like the psalm in the consecration ceremony, it is divided up to form question and answer and is sung antiphonally:

Question
Quem quaeritis in sepulchro Christicolae?
[Whom do you seek in the sepulchre, O Christians?]

Answer
Jesu Nazarenum crucifixum, O caelicolae.
[Jesus of Nazareth who was crucified, O heavenly one.]

Questioner
Non est hic, surrexit sicut praedixerat.
Ite, nunciate quia surrexit de sepulchro.
[He is not here; he is risen as he foretold.
Go, announce that he is risen from the dead.]

To show how this extended trope developed into a play we shall turn our attention to England during the reign of the Saxon King Edgar. There is a known historical background to this particular example which, because it reveals the sort of problem which beset the Church in those days, I shall briefly relate.

Edgar reigned during the years 959–975, a period of peace following upon the terrible wars with the invading Danish Vikings. It was the policy of Edgar to re-establish in England the monastic life which had fallen sadly into decay during the Danish wars, as a result partly of the destruction of the monasteries by the pagan Danes and partly of neglect by the Saxons under the cruel pressure of invasion. It should be remembered that in early mediaeval times the monasteries formed the backbone of Christian culture and learning: hence the importance of what Edgar set out to achieve.

By far the largest part of the work fell upon the shoulders of three great churchmen whose learning, experience, religious inspiration and administrative ability admirably fitted them for the task. These men were: Saint Dunstan, Archbishop of Canterbury: Saint Oswald, Bishop of Worcester and later Archbishop of York; and Saint Ethelwold, Bishop of Winchester. It is with the last of the three that we as students of theatre and drama are directly concerned.

Between the years 963 and 975 Edgar set up a council at Winchester to consider by what religious custom the monks of England should discipline their lives. Because the custom, or 'monastic rule' as it is frequently called, was to be commonly applied throughout the land it was necessary that agreement upon it also should be general. When agreement had been finally reached it was left to Ethelwold to draw up the terms of the rule in detail. The name by which Ethelwold's work is known is the *Regularis Concordia*, which we should roughly translate as 'The Code or Rule Reached by General Agreement'.

Now, included in Ethelwold's Code is a detailed direction governing the way in which the Easter trope of the *Quem Quaeritis* should be conducted. So important is this direction that I shall quote it in full.

If we bear in mind our picture of the complete theatre of the church we should find no difficulty in bringing the scene vividly to life.

While the third lesson is being chanted, let four brethren vest themselves; of whom let one, vested in an alb [a white garment reaching to the feet] enter as if to take part in the service, and let him without being observed approach the place of the sepulchre, and there, holding a palm in his hand, let him sit down quietly. While the third responsory is being sung let the remaining three follow, all of them vested in copes [long cloaks] and carrying in their hands censers filled with incense; and slowly, in the manner of seeking something, let them come before the place of the sepulchre. These things are done in imitation of the angel seated in the sepulchre, and of the women coming with spices to anoint the body of Jesus. When, therefore, that one seated shall see the three, as if straying about and seeking something, approach him, let him begin in a sweet voice of medium pitch to sing:

Whom do you seek in the sepulchre, O followers of Christ?

When he has sung this to the end, let the three respond in unison:

Jesus of Nazareth who was crucified, O celestial one.

To whom that one:

He is not here; he is risen, just as he foretold.
Go, announce that he is risen from the dead.

At this word of command let the three turn themselves into the choir, saying:

Alleluia! The Lord is risen to-day,
The strong lion, the Christ, the Son of God.
Give thanks to God, huzza!

This said, let the former, again seating himself, as if recalling them, sing the anthem:

41

> Come and see the place where the Lord was laid.
> Alleluia! Alleluia!

And saying this, let him rise, and let him lift the veil and show them the place bare of the cross but only the cloths laid there with which the cross was wrapped. [*Note* The cross would by now have been restored to its normal position.] Seeing which, let the three set down the censers which they carried into the sepulchre, and let them take up the cloth and spread it out before the eyes of the clergy; and, as if making known that the Lord had risen and was not now therein wrapped, let them sing this anthem:

> The Lord is risen from the sepulchre,
> Who for us hung upon the cross.

And let them place the cloth upon the altar. The anthem being ended, let the Prior, rejoicing with them at the triumph of our King in that, having conquered death he arose, begin the hymn:

> *Te deum laudamus* —   [We praise thee, O God —]

This begun, let all the bells chime out together.

Here, of course, we have a very important document which clearly reveals the flowering of a short but complete play from the musical stem of the Easter trope. In the first place, there is a fully developed plot which begins on a note of grief when the women come in search of the body of their crucified leader and master. A climax is rapidly reached when the women are confronted by the divine being who announces the resurrection of Jesus and offers proof in the shape of the cloths which the risen God has cast aside. Grief changes to joy as the women comprehend the miracle that has taken place, and the whole audience joins in the singing of a great song of praise. In the second place, we have actors consciously performing parts in character and expressing themselves, in movement as well as in voice, according to the requirements of the plot. Suddenly the theatre of ritual has become the theatre of the play. The ritualistic garments of priests are now the 'fit up' costumes of actors and the deeply religious symbols of sepulchre and shrouding cloth now serve as stage properties.

But what we have before us represents more than the script of a play. It is a complete scenario with full directions for the actors and stage effects, all of which are aimed at audience reaction or response. We are able to measure the degree of care that was taken to create and maintain a stage 'illusion' and we are made conscious of the thought that was given to the 'timing' of the performance. As for the theme, this was in itself a sufficient source of 'wonder', that essential ingredient of all true theatre, but it was the dramatic presentation which made the 'wonder' popular. Nor, in considering the theatrical response to this very short play, should we fail to note the effectiveness of the songs, particularly the great song of praise known as the *Te deum* which has been throughout the centuries the established song of thanksgiving for all Christian people and for all Christian nations. The singing of the *Te deum* would in any case have formed a normal part of the Easter service, though doubtless the majority of the Saxon congregation would have been deaf to the Latin. Coming as it did, however, at the end of an acted play, and attended as it was by the ringing out of the bells, it could hardly have failed to excite the feelings even of the dullest Saxon present. This, indeed, was the stated intention of St Ethelwold.

Once the 'dramatic idea' had taken hold in the theatre of the church, the dramatic art began to develop both in scope and in magnitude. It is impossible to trace precisely the course of dramatic development within the early mediaeval Church because of the gaps which occur in the documentary evidence available to us. A manuscript of the thirteenth century, for example, coming to light in an ancient monastery or perhaps in a mediaeval cathedral, could possibly reveal what appears to be a new and exciting development in character presentation or stage setting or thematic material: but it is always possible that sooner or later, an even earlier manuscript might come to light showing that the fresh development actually took place long before the thirteenth century. Difficulties of this sort are apt to put pitfalls in the way of the student as his studies become more advanced. Nevertheless, sufficient evidence has been gathered from various sources in Europe to acquaint us generally with the way in which the plays accumulated in number and in scope. The chief focal points around which the plays seemed to group themselves and develop were the festivals of Easter and Christmas. For the purpose of explaining the sort of process at work throughout Europe during the period, I shall choose a number of plays which were performed at Christmas. The reader should bear in mind, however, that we shall be dealing only with what was typical and that no attempt will be made at a complete survey. The legends to which we shall be referring are those of the New Testament, Chapters 1 and 2 of St Matthew, and Chapter 2 of St Luke.

The stories of Christ's birth as related by St Matthew and St Luke differ in a number of ways, though each one is complementary to the other. The account given by St Matthew tells of the Magi (the Three Kings or Wise Men) who, led by a star, come in search of the infant Christ. They interrupt their journey to call at the court of Herod, the king of Judaea, where they enquire about the child. Herod is curious, and on being told that the child destined to rule over Israel would, according to the ancient prophets, be born in Bethlehem, plots to kill the young Jesus. With fair words he sends the Magi to Bethlehem, pressing them to visit him on their return so that they may inform him as to the child's whereabouts. Still guided by the star, the Magi continue on their way to Bethlehem where they find Jesus. Having worshipped the child, they present him with rich gifts of gold, frankincense and myrrh. But they are prevented from re-visiting Herod by a dream which warns them to return home by another route. Herod, hearing how he has been cheated, orders the slaughter of all the children in Bethlehem who are under two years old (the 'Slaughter of the Innocents') but Jesus escapes, having been carried into Egypt by his mother Mary and his foster father, Joseph.

The account given by St Luke tells how Joseph with his wife journeyed from Nazareth to Bethlehem and how Jesus was born there, having to be placed in the manger of a stable because there was 'no room for them in the inn'. St Luke goes on to relate how an angel appeared to certain shepherds who were guarding their flock in the night. He tells of the fear which overcame the shepherds at the glorious apparition and how the angel, having calmed them, imparts the news of the birth of Jesus, the 'Saviour who is Christ the Lord'. The angel directs that the shepherds shall go in search of the child, upon which the heavens open to disclose the heavenly multitude singing: 'Glory to God in the highest and on earth peace, goodwill towards men.' The shepherds then go to Bethlehem where they find Jesus lying in a manger just as the angel had foretold. Filled with wonder they go to spread the news of Christ's birth.

Now, the reader with a discerning eye for the potentials of stage production will not be slow to detect the possibilities that exist in both of these accounts for theatrical and dramatic development:

nor will he or she fail to observe that the possibilities offered are quite distinct in each case. St Matthew's narrative provides an immediate appeal to the sense of conflict and danger while that of St Luke offers the prospect of exciting spectacle together with a dramatic contrast between high magnificence and heavenly power on the one hand and humble poverty on the other. We shall see how, in what might seem to have been a step by step process, though there is no firm documentary proof that it was, each of the narratives was theatrically exploited along these lines until they merged in a single play of exceptional interest and power. But first we have to turn our attention to the symbols which, like the cross in the Easter *Quem Quaeritis*, played a vital part in the dramatization of both narratives.

There were two symbolical representations which were important to the Christmas celebration in mediaeval times. These were the crib or manger, which in form was more or less the same as the Christmas crib which we see in many churches and occasionally shop windows during the Christmas season today, and the star or *corona* which was hung high in the chancel of the church. Both symbols seem to have been used ceremonially at a very early date. The crib dates back probably to the third century and it was in fairly common use five centuries later. The star was a circle either of wood or metal upon which lighted candles were mounted. As we shall see, it evolved in due course into an interesting piece of stage machinery.

We shall begin with a very short play—hardly a play at all in fact—which was based upon the account of the Nativity given by St Luke and which had become customary at the cathedral of Padua by the thirteenth century.

The crib is placed in the middle of the chancel and it contains a doll. Mary the Virgin Mother is also represented by an artificial figure and not acted as she is to be in later plays. Speaking parts are given to four members of the clergy, two of whom represent midwives and stand behind the crib while the others play the part of shepherds. The following dialogue then ensues (note that it begins in precisely the same way as the Easter *Quem Quaeritis*, thus suggesting the trope from which it originally stemmed):

Midwives (to the approaching shepherds)
Whom do you seek in the manger, O shepherds, say.

Shepherds
The Saviour, the Christ, the infant Lord, wrapped in swaddling clothes according to the words of the angel.

Midwives
The infant is here with Mary his mother of whom long ago the prophet Isaiah spoke: 'Behold, a virgin shall conceive and bear a son.' And now as you go forth announce that he is born.

Shepherds, crying out in loud voices
Alleluia! Alleluia! Now we know in very truth that the Christ is born into the world; of whom let all sing, saying with the prophet:
    'Unto us a child is born!'

Obviously this does not take us far beyond a live presentation of a portion of St Luke's text. Two manuscripts from Rouen Cathedral show a spectacular choral embellishment which marks a considerable advance on the play of Padua. The manuscripts come respectively from the fourteenth and fifteenth centuries, though the play which they put on record had probably been in existence for many generations. The text differs very little from that of the Padua play but, like the text of St Ethelwold's *Quem Quaeritis*, it provides a complete scenario which reveals the sort of stage 'illusion' that was aimed at. First, it directs that a manger be prepared at the back of the altar which is to include the figure of Mary. It is then ordered that a boy, 'dressed like an angel, from a lofty place in front of the choir', should announce the birth of Jesus, thus impersonating the angel who appeared to the shepherds. As soon as this is done a number of choir boys appear high in the arched gallery, known as the triforium, above the chancel where they sing 'as though they were angels' the *Gloria in excelsis* [Glory to God in the highest, and on earth peace, goodwill towards men]. The parts of the midwives and shepherds are played by members of the clergy exactly as they are performed in the Padua play but, simple and short though the whole thing is, there is no doubt that the use of the boy choristers to represent angels in the manner directed must have produced a startlingly grand 'illusion' in the imaginations of the congregation or audience.

We now come to plays which are based upon St Matthew's version of the Christmas story. And here we see an entirely fresh development emerging from the liturgy of the Church. In our second chapter we noted that the ritual of the Mass included the

46

Fig. 4   A mediaeval cathedral choir: note the triforium, from
whose shadowed arches the choir boys appeared at
Christmas to represent the angelic choir singing at
Christ's birth

offering of gifts for the poor. This act was performed ceremoniously and it was known as the 'oblation' or 'gift to God'. It seems to have become customary, particularly in the larger churches, on the feast of the Epiphany (the twelfth day after Christmas, and the day set aside to commemorate the journey of the Magi) to associate the oblation with the offerings of the Magi to the infant Christ. This association led to a form of ceremonial procession which included the performance of stage parts and the use of the 'star' or *corona* as an important mechanical stage property. We again look to the cathedral of Rouen for an example of the proceedings which is both simple and very informative. As before with the Rouen Shepherds' play, we rely upon a late manuscript (fourteenth century) which recorded a custom that was already ancient.

We have to imagine a very large cruciform church, that is, a church built in the form of a cross on an east-to-west axis having its arms or 'transepts' extending outwards at right angles to the nave. It should be remembered that the nave would have had no seats to offer any hindrance to the forming of a procession. The star with its candles lit is suspended above the altar.

The ceremony begins with the appearance of the Magi from three different parts of the church. Each is followed by a train of 'servants', who are in fact other members of the clergy, bearing gifts which include the gold, frankincense and myrrh of the three kings. The Magi meet in the central space in front of the chancel, and the following dialogue ensues:

1st King *(Having approached from the east, and pointing with his staff —)*
This star blazes with an exceptional brightness.

2nd King
That shows that the King of Kings is born.

3rd King
Whose coming the prophets foretold long ago.

This piece of dialogue is well worth noting because it seems to have been 'invented' to fit the occasion instead of having sprung from a sung trope.

The kings then embrace and sing the following line of the script together:

Let us go then, and seek him, offering to him the gifts: gold, frankincense and myrrh.

48

Fig. 5   An alabaster panel from Long Melford Church, Suffolk, showing the Adoration of the Three Kings: the panel seems to reflect a performance of a Nativity in the chancel, as described below in the account of the Rouen play of the Magi

Whereupon the cantor (the leader of the choir) begins a series of responses while the procession of gift-bearers forms up in the nave. These sung responses deliver an account of the journey of the Magi from the East, led by the Star, and of their visit to the court of Herod. In form it is very much like the recitative of an opera or an oratorio.

Once the procession is assembled in the nave and the Magi have placed themselves at its head, it is directed that the *corona* should be raised by means of its pulley to simulate the moving of the Star while the Magi, as though following it, lead the procession to the altar where a statue of the Virgin Mother has been placed in readiness. As the procession moves the Magi take up the singing of the following stirring anthem:

'There shall come a star out of Jacob, and a man shall arise out of Israel, and he shall break in pieces all the leaders of the gentiles and the whole earth shall be his possession.'

At this point two midwives appear, their parts played by members of the clergy, and stand one on each side of the altar. As the procession advances they turn to the Magi, and the following dialogue is delivered:

Midwives
Who are these who, approaching us led by a star, bear strange things?

Magi
We whom ye see are the Kings of Tharsis, and of Arabia, and of Saba, bearing gifts to the Christ, the new-born king, the Lord, whom we, led by a star, are come to worship.

Midwives (Drawing aside a curtain to display the crib —)
See, here is the boy whom ye seek. Now hasten to worship him, for he is the redeemer of the world.

Each of the Magi then speaks to the child in salutation, at the same time offering his gift which he takes from his attendant 'servant'. And here custom is again exploited to produce at least the shadow of a further dramatic sequence. For it was the practice, following upon the oblation, for the giver to bow in silent prayer. As the Magi do so, a boy chorister appears to perform the part of a messenger angel. He addresses the kings as though, instead of being at prayer, they are asleep, and warns them to avoid the court of King Herod on their return journey. This, in effect, is the end of the play.

Clearly, the Rouen manuscript reveals a consciousness of the dramatic potentials of St Matthew's narrative. It puts into character six parts, if we include the impersonation of the messenger angel; it 'invents' dialogue throughout; and it anticipates the drama of Herod's plot. How these potentials were exploited to the full to produce a play of considerable length and dramatic force, and in the costume of the time instead of 'fit up' ecclesiastical costume, is brought to light in a much earlier manuscript of the twelfth century which was discovered at the Abbey of Saint-Benoit-sur-Loire in France.

The play in question bears the title *Herod* and it blends together in a manner which shows genuine stagecraft a number of events which appear in the narratives both of St Matthew and St Luke. It begins, as the Rouen Shepherds' Play begins, with the appearance high above the chancel of choristers who collectively act the part of the Heavenly Host. Here, however, the shepherds, who appear below, act their terror, at which the leader of the choir utters the comforting words of the messenger angel, as they are written in the Gospel of St Luke, and proclaims the birth of Jesus. The direction given in the script continues:

And suddenly let all the multitude with the Angel say:
Glory to God in the highest, and on earth peace and goodwill to men! Alleluia! Alleluia!

What follows is a particularly interesting piece of development. For the shepherds, having spoken among themselves in character, go in search of the manger 'which shall have been prepared at the doors of the monastery'. It is probable that a special reason existed for placing the crib in this position rather than in the chancel of the church but this need not concern us. The important thing is that it called for the movement of actors from one scene or 'set' to another, a practice that was to become very common in the mediaeval theatre as a whole. It provided a situation, moreover, which was suitable for the joining of the play of the Shepherds to that of the Magi.

The shepherds make their way to the crib where they are greeted by two midwives who challenge them with the question, 'Whom seek ye?—' etc. On being told by the shepherds that they come in search of 'the Saviour, the Christ, the infant Lord,' the midwives point to the crib with the figure of Mary by its side, and say:

The little one is here with Mary his mother, of whom long ago the prophet Isaiah said: 'Behold, a virgin shall conceive and bear a son.'

When the shepherds have acclaimed the child and have fallen prostrate in worship, a direction is given in the text of the manuscript which is of considerable interest to the student. It says:

Afterwards, as they rise to their feet, let them call upon the people standing about to worship the child, saying to the nearby throng:

Come! Come! Come! Let us worship the God, since he alone is our Saviour.

What we are getting here is a very interesting development indeed, because the play itself, having left the great 'picture stage' of the chancel and sanctuary, has suddenly become theatre 'in the round' with the audience gathered closely around the players and the stage 'set'. Here again we have a theatrical development which was to become a major characteristic of the mediaeval stage, and it is well worth remembering that the development was to continue within the theatre of the church itself with a number of 'places' or 'sets' erected at need on opposite sides of the nave.

At this point in our play the theme of the Magi is taken up. The three kings assemble at the altar, approaching from three different parts of the church, and drawn thither by the Star almost exactly in the manner adopted in the Rouen play of the Magi. Unlike the Rouen play, however, the three kings appear to have no following of 'servants' and there is no suggestion of a procession. Instead, as soon as the kings have greeted one another, the Star moves and the three men follow it to the arch of the chancel. Having reached this point they enquire 'of those standing by' where the new-born king of the Jews is to be found. And here we get an important extension of the action of the play to embrace a further part of St Matthew's narrative. For King Herod is made to appear in person surrounded by soldiers and courtiers clad in the clothes of 'young gallants'. The group stand a little apart from the crowd, but Herod hears what is said by the Magi and promptly sends a soldier to bring them before him. He asks them what child it is of whom they speak and they tell him of the child who is born to be a king reigning over other kings of the world. Disturbed by the news, Herod asks the Magi if they really believe in the existence of this child, and on being informed that they do he sends for his scribes, who appear carrying a book. Herod orders the scribes to search in the book for evidence of the birth of the child king. They do so and discover the prophecy that foretells the coming of the Christ, whereupon Herod falls into a rage and, seizing the book from the scribes, dashes it to the ground. In a well-contrived piece of side-play Herod's son comes forward to offer himself as a champion should his father decide to declare war on the infant usurper, but Herod cunningly sends the Magi on their way, asking them to return and inform him where Jesus is to be found so that he also may go to swear his allegiance.

We are given a change of scene as the Magi, still led by the moving Star, advance along the nave of the church while Herod and his company menacingly wave their swords in the background or, as we should say, 'upstage'. When the kings have gone some distance they are met by the shepherds returning from the crib. The shepherds tell the Magi what they have seen and then depart leaving the latter to continue their journey to the crib, where they offer their gifts and make their obeisance. The play closes with the appearance of an angel to warn the Magi to return home by a different route.

Now, here we have a play of considerable length with a well-defined plot and a cleverly contrived action which makes full use of the theatre of the church. It is a play, moreover, which employs a very large cast dressed in contemporary lay costume and not the 'fit up' ecclesiastical costume of the other plays we have mentioned. Its dialogue is for the most part 'invented' and in character; and, which is very important, apart from the symbols which are the necessary focal points of the play, it reveals only faintly its ritualistic origins. In brief, the dramatic idea has emerged as a complete dramatic form of art.

What needs specially to be noted at the present moment, however, is the fact that this Herod play draws together a number of incidents from two New Testament narratives and presents them as a single dramatic plot. This process seems to have been continuous and, as we have already pointed out, focused mainly upon the great festivals of Christmas and Easter. What it amounted to was the drawing together, as a dramatic and theatrical demonstration or exposition, of all the major events of the Christian legend. For reasons which I have already explained, we are unable to link together all the details of the process. But we do know that its end product lay in the Mystery Cycles of England and of the continent of Europe. These show that the process moved gradually towards a grand design or conception which amounted to no less than the history of the world from its beginning to its end as seen through mediaeval eyes.

A great deal more will be said about the process and the grand conception in a later chapter, but there is still one point that needs to be added before we close this brief survey of the emergence of the dramatic idea. This concerns theatrical popularity.

Before a theatre can take root in a civilization or, indeed, before it can form any part of the civilizing process, it must be popular. This popularity begins with the ritual upon which the drama is founded and it continues with the legends which are chosen for the dramatic themes. The legends of the mediaeval theatre were the legends of Christianity, and if the modern student of mediaeval theatre wishes to attempt to leap the gap of the ages and enter as far as he can into the minds of the audiences who regarded the theatre of their times as a 'wonder' and a 'show', he must appreciate the essential popularity of the Christian legend. In the last chapter I pointed out the simplicity and absoluteness with which mediaeval people accepted the Christian legend. This means that not only did everyone accept the legend, but every individual knew that every other individual accepted it too. It is only when this happens that we can say that a belief is popular or, in other words, common to all people. Fortunately for the student, there are many means of access to the reality of this popular acceptance in mediaeval times. Its literature is saturated with it, and so is its fine art. Most intimately connected with the theatre, however, are the carvings in stone and wood and the paintings which, as I have already said, are to be found in a good state of preservation in many mediaeval churches today. A large proportion of these craft works are in themselves dramatic; indeed, so closely do many of them resemble scenes from mediaeval plays that it is impossible to tell whether a stone mason or a wood carver or a glass painter took his inspiration from a play he had seen or whether he himself, through some flight of fancy or burst of robust humour, had influenced the mind of the playwright. Such paintings and carvings are a constant source of help, not only to the student, but to producers and designers who are in any way connected with the production of a mediaeval play. The simple fact is that the arts and crafts of the mediaeval age were as capable of reflecting the 'dramatic idea' as was the stage itself, and this was largely because of the universal acceptance of the Christian legend as a common source as well as an interpretation of civilized life.

4

THE SPIRIT OF IRREVERENCE

Everything that we have dealt with so far reflects the reverent observance of the rites or, as they are usually called, the 'liturgy' of the Church, and of the plays that developed from those rites. We have now to ask whether the observances were always as solemn and as reverent as a modern Christian or, for that matter, non-Christian would expect. The answer is that they were not, and that there were occasions when they were treated with the outrageous disrespect which we in our own day normally associate with theatrical burlesque of the coarsest kind. How this came about, and the sort of riotous fun-making that took place within the church building itself, I shall now try to explain; and the best way to go about it will be to draw an imaginary picture of the kind of scene which appears to have been common at Christmas-time, particularly in the larger churches of the greater part of Europe, including England.

In creating our picture we shall have to bear in mind that it is based for the most part upon the evidence gained from the efforts of outraged dignitaries of the Church—usually bishops, but some-times the Pope himself—to suppress or restrain scenes of this nature. In other words, we shall rely upon orders which have been preserved saying that this or that shall not be done. The overall result will be an imaginary, composite picture of events which, while they certainly occurred, did not necessarily do so in a single specified place or exactly in the sequence given.

Imagine, then, the interior of a large church, say a cathedral, at the hour of Vespers (Evensong) on a certain day during the twelve days of Christmas. The chancel is packed with members of the clergy who sit in three rows on either side. In the back row we have the senior clergy: the Dean, the sub-Dean, the archdeacons, canons, and so on. In the second row sit clergy of lower status, while in the first row sit those of the lowest status of all: the sub-deacons. If choir boys are present they will be seated in front of the first row of the clergy.

The service of Vespers is proceeding as usual; solemn, as we imagine, but with something a little odd about it. The precentor, perhaps, who is there in charge of the choir with his *baculus* or wand of office, shows a certain lack of concentration; and there is an atmosphere of expectancy in the place as though something unusual is about to happen. Probably what is most noticeable is a subtle tenseness in the sub-deacons: a tenseness, not of fear, but that which comes from gleeful anticipation of mischief. The orderly manner of the service, however, goes on unbroken for about one-third of its length, that is, up to the singing of the *Magnificat*.

Now, the *Magnificat* is one of the most solemn and significant hymns or canticles in the Christian liturgy. It was the hymn uttered by Mary the Mother of Jesus when, during her pregnancy, she went to visit her cousin Elizabeth, and it therefore marks an important point in the Christian legend. But there is more to it than this. It is a hymn of thanksgiving and praise to the unseen God and it lays particular stress upon the divine characteristic which brings about the downfall of the powerful and the proud and the uplifting of the poor and oppressed. In other words, it sings in praise of the universal equalizing force or spirit which the ancient Greeks themselves honoured in their recognition of the dreadful sin of *hubris* (pride). The lines of the *Magnificat* that most clearly reflect this spirit are:

He hath put down the mighty from their seats
And hath exalted the humble and meek.

Yet it is here that all the tenseness of anticipation observed in our imaginary scene breaks forth into riotous action. The *Magnificat* is allowed to begin with sufficient solemnity:

Magnificat anima mea Dominum   [My soul doth magnify the Lord]

But on the line 'He hath put down—', etc., the words 'put down' are taken up by the sub-deacons as a cry which soon rises to a positive yell: 'Put down! Put down! Put down!' Still yelling, they leave their stalls and mount to the third row where they seize upon their superiors in status and throw them out, making them descend to the first row while they themselves with joyful ostentation take the higher places. Meanwhile, one of their number (appointed beforehand) approaches the precentor, seizes his wand of office and takes charge.

What follows is a complete travesty of the divine service. All is pandemonium and chaos. The sub-deacons form themselves into a procession and in mock solemnity cense the church—but not with incense. Instead they swing smouldering shoes from side to side, filling the place with the acrid stink of burning, sweaty leather. In what appears to be an appalling mockery of the altar, they eat black puddings there. Then a sermon is given which is not merely a travesty, but bawdy as well, and delivered in a sort of pidgin Latin which makes use of English words with latinized endings.

As time goes on the riot spreads and becomes even more rowdy. Wine and ale are brought into the church porch which becomes crammed with a disorderly mob of boozing men while perhaps a number of sub-deacons march into the streets where they capture a pretty girl (probably one known to have loose morals), mount her on a donkey and carry her in triumph to the altar of the church, as a burlesque upon Joseph's journey with Mary and the infant Jesus into Egypt.

Although, as I have said, this is an imaginary picture which must not be taken as an accurate account of a series of events known to have taken place in a particular church, we do know that such happenings were of regular occurrence at Christmas-time and that they took place on a special day set aside for the sub-deacons. This was the day which came to be known as the Feast of Fools. We shall in a moment look more closely at the matter and try to explain it in flesh-and-blood human terms, but since the word 'burlesque' has already been used, I shall first define the meaning of the word as we shall use it in the present book.

Probably most of us would agree that we like to see things, particularly the 'established order of things', turned upside-down occasionally and that we frequently laugh when they are. The spectacle 'tickles our sense of humour'. What we seem most to enjoy, however, is the turning upside-down of authority, especially when authority becomes self-important, aggressive or in any way over-blown. When I use the word 'burlesque' in these pages I mean the deliberate turning of things upside-down or, as we say, 'topsy-turvy', for the sake of laughter. We therefore regard the Feast of Fools as burlesque because it replaces reverence with irreverence; religion with irreligion; and respect for authority with contempt for it. Each pair of terms, we should note, represents an exact opposite.

Now, it seems that man has always possessed an instinct for burlesque and its companion spirit of irreverence. Certainly burlesque is the surest cure for an overdose of reverence, so it is just as well perhaps that we have it. There are many examples in history of burlesque rituals or rituals in reverse. The ancient Greek Comus (from which our word comedy is derived) is one of these. The dancers of the Comus had the right, which was jealously preserved, to hold important men of the time, and even the gods, up to ridicule. Another well-known burlesque was the Roman *Saturnalia* in which the whole of the social order was turned upside-down when masters changed places with servants and slaves. The *Saturnalia* is very important to us historically because of the influence it has had upon our celebration of Christmas through the ages, despite the efforts of many Christian men to suppress it. Even today, the traces of this Roman festival of December remain in the lighting of candles, the exchange of gifts and the general revelry with which we always associate Christmas. In mediaeval times the pagan appeal was exceedingly strong and the riotous behaviour of the sub-deacons in the Feast of Fools reflected this appeal to a considerable degree.

But it is most probable that the root of the sub-deacons' festival and other Christmas festivals of a similar nature lay in a piece of Christian symbolism that was very solemn and reverent in its intent. In purely Christian terms, the celebration of Christmas was a reminder of a number of things. In the first place, of course, it celebrated the birth of the founder of Christianity. But the birth took place in lowly and squalid circumstances, and herein lay a fundamental principle of the Christian faith. For the whole life of Jesus was characterized by poverty, humility and obedience, and these were the characteristics through which his divine being conquered the whole world, making him King above all kings. What better time could there be to demonstrate the point symbolically; and what better moment could be chosen to introduce a symbolical act than the singing of the *Magnificat* at the point where the chorus tells of the putting down of the mighty from their seats and the raising or exalting of the humble and meek?

Long before we hear any mention of the Feast of Fools, we learn of days set aside during the Christmas festival for priests, middle clergy and boy choristers during which each group in turn is 'exalted' to the high places of the choir. As an additional dignity on such a day, a previously appointed member of the group took the precentor's wand and from that moment 'ruled the choir'. On Innocents Day, for example, the day which commemorated the slaughter of the children of Bethlehem on the orders of Herod, the choir boys, led by a boy-bishop, took their turn. The boy-bishop was allowed to occupy the high chair of the Dean, and he preached a sermon. It seems, however, that unruliness of one sort or another crept into each of these festivals and it is more than possible that the sub-deacons were largely responsible for it.

Taken altogether, the sub-deacons were a pretty ignorant lot who were held very much in contempt by their more literate superiors. Moreover, it fell to them to perform all the menial and less savoury duties connected with the living-quarters of the cathedral clergy, which meant that their standing amongst the cathedral fraternity was little better than that of servants who were given scant encouragement to respect their betters. Here, if anywhere, was fertile soil for the growth and flourishing of burlesque. For if authority, having asserted itself for the greater part of the year with contempt for the underdog, decides in a sudden fit of humility to say 'On this day of Christmas you shall be raised from the status of underdog to that of topdog taking precedence over me because God works in that way,' it is hardly surprising if the underdog refuses to behave according to the pattern set for him. He will most likely 'burlesque' his part and accept the gesture with an irreverent gusto and enthusiasm which are the reverse of the humility and gratitude expected. We do not know that this was in fact the case but, human nature being what it is, it seems more than possible. One thing that we do know for certain is that at the end of the twelfth century it was deemed necessary to restrict the cries of *Deposuit!* [Put down!] to five in number.

Another outlet for the mediaeval spirit of irreverence appears in the form which we should now describe as rude parody. And here again it seems that the sub-deacons were mainly responsible.

There were various parts of the Church liturgy (see the Glossary of Terms) which called for the reading of passages from the Old and New Testaments. It became the practice on certain occasions to insert into the text short passages, or tropes, of simple doggerel rhyme, the serious purpose of which was to impress the lesson on the minds of the ignorant and semi-literate. A well-known scholar of the nineteenth century, J. M. Neale, has translated a passage of this kind into English. Here is a part of it with the tropes in italics:

> He that fears the Lord will do good,
>> *And when this evil life is past*
>> *Receive the King's reward at last.*
> And he that has knowledge of the law shall obtain her,
> And as a mother shall she meet him.
>> *For He is full of love and grace,*
>> *And mercy guards his dwelling place,*
>> *And glory shines around his face.*

The name given to this practice was 'infarcation' which means 'sandwiching in between'.

Now, we should no doubt most of us agree that, while it is a good and worthy thing to convey knowledge to the ignorant, this is a particularly dangerous way of setting about the task. If you 'talk down' to ignorance with childish tum-te-tum rhythm and rhyme, then ignorance will feel that you are patronizing it and resent the fact. It will, moreover, take its revenge and use its native wit to parody your instructive little rhyme with a rude and probably bawdy version of its own. It is hardly necessary to emphasize this point since our own age bristles with examples which reveal the same process at work. What is historically important is that the theatrical word 'farce' is derived from the word 'infarcation' and that the art of farce developed from mediaeval parody.

But, the bawdy 'goings-on' of the sub-deacons apart, mediaeval people seem to have been ready at all times to laugh at the expense of 'holy things' and 'holy personages', just as they were ready to laugh at such prime representatives of evil as the devil and his attendant demons. Sometimes, as a few of the great Miracle plays show, they would laugh at God himself—and when they did, the laughter was often decidedly rude. This is a characteristic that often puzzles the modern student of mediaeval theatre because it seems so much out of keeping with his conception of an audience saturated with Christian doctrine. The problem becomes less difficult, however, when we begin to take into consideration the simple directness of popular mediaeval belief.

We have already referred in the second chapter to the vivid imagery which filled the minds of mediaeval people in their interpretation of Christian history and legend. Let us take a look at some of the more important figures and conceptions that played a direct part in their lives and, so far as we are able, estimate the effect these had, and in consequence their theatrical impact.

God, of course, was universally accepted as the ultimate power; the giver of life and punisher of sin. He was God Omnipotent; the King of Kings and Lord of Lords who was constantly at war with Satan, the Prince of Evil. And because God's war with Satan was for the possession of men's souls, the sense of his presence was intense and vividly familiar and personal. This is most certainly the impression that we get from the Miracle cycles in which God is frequently represented as a living character upon the stage. But the stage image of God is never quite consistent. Sometimes he appears as a benevolent, merciful person, pitying the sufferings of mankind. At other times, as in the Chester play of the *Deluge*, he appears as an angry, destroying tyrant. When, as he frequently does, he appears as the God of Eternity whose thought alone is creation, he is sublimely beautiful.

Now, the very inconsistency of these stage images of God throws a light upon the mediaeval mind. Each image represents a view or aspect of the one thing that all the images of God have in common, namely, absolute authority. This is simply a way of saying that God is made to appear, not 'in the round', which would hardly be possible, but as an intensely familiar caricature of a *person* in authority. By looking at the matter in this way we are able to make common ground with the minds of mediaeval people in comparing their reactions to personal authority with our own. How often, we have to ask, do we see the people who wield any sort of authority over ourselves, be they parents or teachers or our 'bosses' at work, absolutely as they are or 'in the round'? Most of us probably would admit on reflection that we do so very rarely, even when they are our parents, and that we most commonly saddle them with an image which changes in accordance with the way in which their authority is felt. When they are benevolent and loving we see them as friends and champions: when they are angry and oppressive we are apt to see them as tyrants. In either case what we see is a caricature, although we often believe that we are seeing the whole person—for the moment, at least. What do we do, then, about the person who appears as a tyrant and whose tyranny we fear? Obviously there are individual answers to this question, but we should all probably agree that a very common one is to do as we are told for fear of the consequences of rebellion, and to cheek the tyrannous one behind his back.

This certainly seems to have been a favourite solution among mediaeval Christians. We have already referred to the angry punishing God of the Chester *Deluge*. To mediaeval people he represented an aspect of God which had to be feared and, whenever human flesh and blood could rise to the occasion—which seems not to have been remarkably often—strictly obeyed. But, as we shall see, they often cheeked him or, as it were, thumbed their noses behind his back, and they loved to see him similarly treated by others.

Finally, something needs to be said about the mediaeval sense of irreverence when applied to Satan and his attendant demons. Here, in a way, the reaction of mockery and laughter seems to have been against the tyranny of evil and its consequences. Devils play a large part in popular mediaeval humour, both on the stage and elsewhere. This does not mean that mediaeval people treated the powers of darkness lightly or with less respect than they treated the powers of Heaven. These devils were ugly, vile beasts who were the inhabitants of the fiery pit of Hell, the place of unending, unspeakable torture to which all souls would inevitably be condemned without the redeeming mercy of their God. Their familiar presence was, in consequence, a continual menace, for they always struck through the material and fleshly lusts of mankind. Much of the laughter gained at the expense of the Devil and his minions, therefore, was of the catch-as-catch-can type, in itself a form of child-like irreverence pointing to the simple uninvolved acceptance that characterizes mediaeval Christian belief. The same images of evil, too, are often found as the agents of social and personal satire. Plate 4A shows a typical example of laughter of this nature, in which a devil is seen carrying off an ale-wife who has been caught giving short measure. Note that the woman is being carried towards the mouth of Hell which is represented by a dragon's mouth just as it was upon the stage of the day. To us the carving possibly appears as a simple piece of mediaeval fun—a light social satire of the time. So, doubtless, it was intended to be. But behind the fun there lay the terrifying and familiar reality from which the mind escaped only through the agency of irreverent humour.

5

THE THEATRE OF
THE PEOPLE

1. THE TRANSITION FROM LATIN TO THE COMMON TONGUE

So far, we have dealt only with the theatre of the church and the plays which were developed for performance within its walls. Many of these plays were, as we have seen, grandly spectacular. They were also essentially musical, firmly connected with Christian ritual, and significantly co-existent with seasonal festivals. To that extent they were popular, even wonderful. But they were still exclusively a function of the Church which meant that they were performed by the clergy within the walls of the church building and delivered throughout in the Latin tongue. What we have to deal with now is the great period of change which saw the transference of the play from the confines of the church to the open air; the passing of the actor's role from the hands of the clergy to those of the laity; the complete taking over of the responsibility for the production of plays by crafts and other guilds and by special societies formed for the purpose; and, most important of all, the rendering of the plays into the common language of the day.

The process of change was universal throughout Europe. It was also very slow and gradual, lasting from about the middle of the twelfth century to the early years of the fourteenth century. It was a process, moreover, which involved the addition of new plays and the moulding of themes of plays dealing with the Christian legend into a complete dramatic whole, known as the 'cycle'. The actual course of development is far from clear in places, and many of its details are the result of enlightened guesswork on the part of modern scholars. Still, a firm pattern exists, and the reader who wishes to trace it with a greater degree of closeness than we shall be able to achieve here should consult Sir Edmund Chambers's *The Mediaeval Stage*, Volume II, chapters xx and xxi.

Plate 1   The mediaeval idea of God the Creator and Architect of the Universe: God is seen in the act of creation, with Heaven above him and the flames of Hell, or the Netherworld, below.

From the Holkham Picture Book Bible

Plate 2A (Above left)

The simple but imposing two-cell Saxon church at Worth in Sussex, showing the sanctuary, sanctuary arch and nave

Plate 2B (Above right)

The exterior of the great apse or sanctuary at Worth

Plate 2C (Left)

The Norman three-cell church of St Mary's at Kilpeck in Hereford-shire, showing the apsidal sanctuary, chancel and nave

Plate 3A   (Left)

The opening in the nave at St Peter's Church, Iver, Buckinghamshire: this opening gave access to the rood loft where the cross or rood, the symbol of Christ's body and crucifixion, was erected high above the nave as the dominant feature of the church.

Plate 3B   (Right)

The rood loft was reached by means of stairs cut into the nave wall: the half-ruinous stairs at St Peter's, Iver, are now sadly redundant reminders of a vividly dramatic past.

Plates 4A (Above) and 4B (Below)
Two misericords from St Laurence's Church at Ludlow, Shropshire
A, above   The devil is seen carrying off a dishonest ale-wife who
has habitually given short measure and is obviously, therefore, a candi-
date for Hell in the eyes of the wood-carver.
B, below   Woman the temptress: two gallants are seen in pursuit
of her, apparently attracted by the fashionable head-dress and oblivious
of the evil nature depicted in her countenance.

Plate 5 The Expulsion from Eden: Adam and Eve, their nakedness covered, are driven from Paradise by the Archangel Michael. Note the 'historical' effect achieved by showing, above, the crime, or sin, which led to the expulsion. Time is ignored.

From the Holkham Picture Book Bible

Plate 6　　Joseph's Trouble: illustrated here is the anger of Joseph, the foster-father of Jesus, when on returning home after a long absence he finds that Mary is pregnant. He grasps her by the abdomen and demands to know the name of the man responsible.

From the Holkham Picture Book Bible

Plate 7   The Last Judgement: a typical 'doom'. The end of the world has come and Christ sits in judgement over all men and women. The redeemed are welcomed into Heaven while the rejected are chained by devils and conducted to the eternal pains of Hell.

From the Holkham Picture Book Bible

Plate 8   Death and the Cardinal: a painted wooden panel at Hexham Abbey in Northumberland. Death is depicted as the grim unseen striker who reduces the great and the humble alike to the final equality of the grave, beyond which all men depend upon the ultimate justice and mercy of God.

In the twelfth century plays began to appear in England and Europe, parts of which—sometimes no more than a few lines—were written in the native tongue. Many of these plays had little or no attachment to actual Church ceremony, though they were performed in the church and dealt with Christian legend. Typical of these were three plays written by the wandering scholar and poet, Hilarius (*fl. c.* 1125), who chose for his themes the Raising of Lazarus; a legendary incident from the life of St Nicholas; and the history of the prophet, Daniel. Hilarius's play about the popular St Nicholas (the original Santa Claus) is one of many plays dealing with the lives and miracles of saints which began to appear during this period. Its theme is humorous and concerns a wealthy heathen named Barbarus who, having to go upon a journey, wishes to leave his wealth in a safe place. Stupidly, he stows all his goods into a chest which he leaves at the foot of a statue of St Nicholas, praying the saint to care for it until his return. Thieves, however, passing the place within which the statue stands, observe that the door is open and enter. They find the chest and rob it of its contents. Barbarus on his return discovers his loss and vents his anger upon the statue to which he delivers a sound whipping. Grieved by this treatment, the statue comes to life, seeks out the thieves and threatens them with exposure to the authorities unless they return their booty to its rightful owner. The robbers, terrified at the threat, promptly obey, and the heathen Barbarus in gratitude to the saint becomes converted to Christianity.

This comical little play is written for the most part in rhymed Latin. But the lines in which Barbarus makes his most dramatic and amusing exclamations are written in Norman French, a language common to both England and France at that time.

What was the most decisive step, however, in the true popularization of Christian drama is represented by the play known as *Le Mystère d'Adam* which probably appeared very shortly after the time of Hilarius. The play is written almost throughout in an Anglo-Norman dialect: and this is by no means its most important feature. It was originally designed for performance on a composite group of stages erected in a large city square and in front of an important church, the porch of which was used as the 'heavenly region' in its general scenic scheme. The stage directions are exceedingly detailed and elaborate and show to what extent the skills of stage design and construction had developed even at this early period. It is required, for example, that the Paradise scene should be furnished with cloths and curtains of silk and provided with masses of fragrant flowers and trees with hanging fruit in order to give the 'likeness of a most delicate spot'. Clear directions are also given as to the costume of the actors, their demeanour when acting their parts, and the pace and enunciation of their stage delivery. Adam, for instance, must be well trained and must be neither too quick nor too slow in taking up his cues. All the characters must speak 'in a composed manner' and must be careful to fit their gestures to the requirements of the action. The importance of stage directions of this nature will not be missed by the enthusiastic student who wishes to learn as much as possible about the skills of stage presentation and acting in the mediaeval period, and he or she will be well advised to study the full translated text of the stage directions of the *Adam* play given by Sir Edmund Chambers in *The Mediaeval Stage*, Volume II, pages 80–82. The introduction by Professor Studer to his Anglo-Norman edition of *Le Mystère d'Adam* published by the Manchester University Press will also be of considerable use.

But what for many is the most notable thing about *Le Mystère d'Adam* is its action. This consists of three parts or acts, namely: the Fall of Man and his casting out from Paradise; the Killing of Abel by his brother Cain (the First Murder); and a procession of prophets of the Old Testament who foretold the coming of the Saviour of Mankind, the latter scene or act being incomplete. We are thus presented with a dramatic sequence, mainly in the native tongue, which covers a considerable part of the Old Testament story: and it is in this that the tremendous importance of the play lies.

We have already seen how, in the theatre of the church, groups of plays developed around the festivals of Christmas and Easter, and how these plays dealt with the birth and sacrificial death of Jesus. But the common theme of these plays was the uplifting of Man to a state of divine love and grace through the birth of God in the Flesh who, after his crucifixion, was to rise again to rule mankind. The dark history of Man between the time of his fall and the day of his redemption nevertheless played an important part in the mediaeval mind, and this too called for dramatic representation. *Le Mystère d'Adam* was not, of course, the first play to do this.

There were already plays or processions in Latin which introduced certain of the prophets who foretold the coming of Christ. The early history of these plays, which are known collectively by the Latin name of *Prophetae*, is too complicated and remote to be dealt with here, but it should be noted that the plays evolved as a part of the liturgy of the Church, largely to illustrate lessons, and that their 'conflict' lay almost exclusively in argument or debate.

What the *Adam* play did was to present a considerable part of the Old Testament legend in a public place, in the native language, and in a manner which was to remain popular throughout the mediaeval age. For, as we shall see, the method of mounting a composite series of plays on a multiple stage, having a number of scenes or sub-stages erected upon its floor, and having the action taking place in, around and between the sub-stages as required, became the approved method of Miracle play production throughout Europe and in some parts of England too.

We do not know exactly how many stages or, rather, sub-stages were called for in the *Adam* play because its text is not complete. This does not matter, however. We know from the detailed stage directions that at least three sub-stages must have existed and we know precisely the sort of action that took place between them. God, for example, appears as a living, speaking 'Figure' who brings forward Adam and Eve and introduces them to Paradise, granting them the enjoyment of all except the forbidden fruit of the Tree of Knowledge. Then God retires to the Heavenly Region (the church porch where, presumably, the choir is situated). Adam and Eve then enter Paradise, and as they do so Satan and his accompanying devils emerge from the sub-stage of the Mouth of Hell to run about the stage, which is at street level, menacing the onlookers—doubtless to the latter's half-terrified delight—and through mime and gesture tempting Eve to eat of the forbidden fruit. Satan then addresses Adam directly and tries to tempt him but is sharply rebuffed. Returning to the hell's mouth, Satan gathers his devils about him in conference and then approaches Eve. But Eve shows reluctance and Adam speaks to her angrily for listening to the tempter. Finally, Satan appears as a serpent and this time succeeds in tempting Eve, who in turn tempts Adam; he also eats of the delicious fruit to make the 'fall' complete. God appears and Adam and Eve hide themselves in shame. They are cast out of Paradise and an angel with a flaming sword is posted at the gate.

67

We can see from this partial description of the action how completely flexible was this type of 'fixed' stage, and how easily the attention of the audience could be transferred from one 'region' to the other. Even the technology associated with the modern cinema could hardly do more. As we move on through *Le Mystère d'Adam* we are able to perceive the potentials of its methods of staging to an even greater degree. For Adam and Eve, once they are cast out of Paradise, are depicted as mortal earthly people having to labour for their keep. They are shown tilling the soil with spade and hoe, wearily and with longing glances in the direction of Paradise. To add to their grief, devils come in their absence and plant thorns and thistles in the midst of their crop. This later scene may have called for a further sub-stage, but it seems more likely that the ground level or stage floor represented the whole of the 'earthly region'. The same sort of thing probably applied to the scene required for the second act or play in the series, *The Killing of Abel*. Here, according to the stage directions, two great stones are prepared beforehand on which Cain and Abel are to offer their individual sacrifices.

One thing further needs to be said about *Le Mystère d'Adam*. Never is the audience allowed to forget the sway of Satan and his host of devils over mankind after the fall of Adam and Eve from divine grace. The devils are everywhere, as we have seen, playing their grim part in every scene and even making sallies amongst the onlookers. But their dramatic significance receives still greater emphasis as we see them carrying off into Hell all earthly people, 'good' as well as 'bad'. Adam and Eve, Cain and Abel, and the prophets in their turn: all go the same way without regard to their virtues or vices. This, of course, was in accordance with Christian theology, but we have to look at the matter from the theatrical viewpoint. In doing so, we see in anticipation the completion of the Miracle cycles which dramatized in a wholly popular theatre the coming of Christ, the redemption of Man, and the ultimate separation of the good souls from the evil at the end of the world.

The same double process of the drawing together of themes in a dramatic series and the rendering of the plays into the common language of the people went on in Germany and England, though in the latter country actual proof in the way of texts is scarce. This is because of the breaking up and partial destruction of monastic libraries in England at the time of the Reformation. A manuscript, however, known as the Shrewsbury Fragments, does exist, which shows the complete process at work in a most interesting way. It contains the fragments of three short plays which deal respectively with the visit of the shepherds to the child Jesus, the visit of the Three Maries to the sepulchre, and the appearance of Christ to the disciples, Luke and Cleophas, after his resurrection. The manuscript, which was discovered by the mediaeval scholar, Professor Skeat, sets out in English the parts for one actor only together with his cues, so that we have, for example:

> *2nd Shepherd*
> . . . not rave.
>
> *3rd Shepherd*
> Yon brightness will us bring
>   Unto that blissful bower;
> For solace shall we sing
>   To* seek our Saviour.   [*As we]

To add to the interest of the manuscript there are passages of narrative or recitative written in Latin and set to music, thus indicating that the plays were intended for performance in a church.

But the rendering of these plays into the common language of the people and their accumulation into groups were not in themselves sufficient to bring into being a coherent series of plays like a Miracle cycle. There had to be a change in the time of performance in order to bring the whole body of plays dealing with the Christian legend together. Once the practice of performing festival plays in the street had taken root, it was a simple matter, as well as a natural wish, to shift their performance to a season of the year when the weather was most likely to be favourable. The adoption of this practice seems to have been gradual but it was greatly assisted in England particularly, by the institution of the feast of *Corpus Christi*. This great festival of the Church was finally established in the year 1311, and the day set aside for its celebration was the Thursday after Trinity Sunday which meant that it had to take place either in May or June.

The central motive of the feast of Corpus Christi was the adoration of the consecrated Host (the Body of Christ) which was carried with great pomp from the church for display before the people. It was an event which, in a highly colourful age like the fourteenth century, must have presented a magnificent spectacle, particularly in the larger towns and cities where the higher clergy were joined in procession by the town or city corporation and the officials of the craft guilds. There are records which show how people flocked from the countryside to cities like York and Norwich to share in the spirit of festival and holiday that prevailed. Affairs of state, even those involving acts of war, were interrupted in order that kings, queens, princes and other high personages could attend.

In thinking of the festival itself we have to imagine, if we can, the sheer theatricality of the scene in a great town as the representatives of the people, with their ceremonial gowns and badges of office, and with their banners emblazoned with the arms of the craft guilds, joined in the procession with the clergy in their richly embroidered vestments. This was the colourful and exciting atmosphere in which the great Miracle cycles finally emerged as a possession of the people, administered by the town and city corporations and financed, rehearsed and performed by the craft guilds.

We do not know exactly how the Miracle plays, or Mystery plays as they are frequently called, got into the hands of the craft guilds. Nor have we certain knowledge of the date and place of performance of the first complete cycle. The obscurity of these matters is largely due to the fact that the play scripts which have survived all show signs of alteration and addition which indicate an earlier original. I shall have something to say presently on the subject of dates, though we can leave speculation to others. It will be useful, however, to observe two points which relate to the subject of the taking over by the craft guilds of responsibility for the production and performance of plays based on the Christian legend. The first is that the craft guilds of the period were in very close contact with the Church. This was a natural relationship in view of the universal acceptance of Christianity. Death and the destiny of a person's immortal soul were serious matters for everyone, the immoral as well as the moral, for which reason it was of vital importance to have Masses said for one's soul after death. The craft guilds undertook to have this done on behalf of their members, and the wealthier of the guilds maintained chantry chapels and priests of their own within the churches of their towns. This is but one of many reasons for the close relationship between an established craft guild and the Church. The second point concerns the ultimate fate of the drama of the Church. It is a fairly common though mistaken view that the Christian drama left the church building for performance in the streets as a direct result of Church disapproval, and this calls for a brief word for the sake of clarification.

There were, of course, many churchmen who throughout the mediaeval period opposed the performance of plays, no matter whether they took place in the church building or in the open air. Nevertheless, in spite of the efforts of reformers, plays continued to be performed in the theatre of the church long after the emergence of the Miracle cycles. It is important to remember that the performance of Christian plays in the open air deprived them of much of the musical background and choral embellishment that only the Church at that time could provide. The retention by the Church of its original plays for performance during the great festivals did much to assist, though in a strictly limited way, in the development of the oratorio at the end of the sixteenth century.

Having said that, we can turn our attention fully to the Miracle cycles, taking to begin with a general view of their composition.

Many scholars describe the cycles as the 'Cosmic Drama of the Middle Ages'. By this they mean that to the audiences of the time the Miracle cycles represented the history of the universe. Now, what the universe amounted to in the mediaeval mind is clearly and simply illustrated in Plate 1. God is seen in the act of creating the world which lies beneath him. He has already created the sun and moon and has given them their places in the sky above the earth. Surrounding the earth is eternity which is represented by Heaven, the place of infinite joy, love and peace, in the upper part, and by the fiery regions of Hell, the place of perpetual evil and torment, in the lower part. Note that the entrance to Hell is symbolized by a dragon's mouth.

All the cycles known to us were based upon a common grand design which began with the war in Heaven in which God, after his victory over the proud and ambitious Lucifer, hurled the rebellious angel into Hell to become its master, Satan. It ended with the final destruction of the world by fire when the living and the dead were called to the Last Judgement. What appeared in between was the history of the world according to the legends of the Old and New Testaments, together with the books which are no longer accepted as authentic parts of the Bible and are known as the Apocrypha.

The cycles that are known to us tend to vary in the number and length of the plays represented, and they also vary to a certain extent in their choice of thematic material. Practically all of them, however, seem to have followed a common skeletal pattern in which the following important events are featured:

1 The Fall of Lucifer
2 The Creation of the World and the Creation and Fall of Man
3 The Murder of Abel by his brother Cain
4 Noah and the Flood
5 The Israelites in Egypt and the giving to Moses of the Ten Commandments
6 The Annunciation or the Divine Conception of Jesus by Mary, and Joseph's 'trouble' in doubting the faithfulness of his wife
7 The Birth of Jesus

Fig. 6   The stage at Valenciennes

8   The Ministry of Jesus; his Betrayal, Trial and Execution (The Passion of Christ)

9   The Resurrection, and the Appearance of Jesus to his Disciples

10   The Ascension (the ascent of Jesus into Heaven)

11   The End of the World and the Last Judgement

By now the reader will have gathered something of the consciousness of the average mediaeval Christian and will not in consequence be surprised to find that the New Testament plays which concern the Redemption of Man form a natural focal point for each cycle, not because of 'literary design', which is lacking in any case, but because of the quantity of plays devoted to the subject. He or she will also occasionally find on reading the plays that a strain of irreverent humour is at times allowed to enter into the proceedings, very often as a consciously confessed piece of mediaeval 'fun making', for, as I hope to show presently, the popular theatre of mediaeval times was a complete theatre in every sense of the term.

It is in the method of theatrical presentation that the first major distinction between the cycles arises. Roughly, the forms of staging fall into two categories: the processional form in which the plays were mounted on 'pageants' or travelling stages which were manually drawn, or as the term went, 'horsed', through the streets for performance at a number of pre-determined stations; and the static form in which the action took place on a multiple fixed stage. The latter form was common on the continent, and it seems to have been frequently employed in England as well. Figure 6 shows a highly elaborate example of a fixed multiple stage which was used for the widely famed Passion play at Valenciennes in 1547, a play which, incidentally, took twenty-five days to perform. It is interesting to see how, even at this late date when scene building had reached an advanced stage of sophistication, the method of presentation is basically the same as it was for *Le Mystère d'Adam* some four hundred years earlier. Nevertheless, the practice of setting sub-stages in line was not always adhered to. In Cornwall, for example, Miracle plays were performed in a circular arena which had scenes or sub-stages erected at its circumference. The principle was the same, however, since the stage floor or 'in-between' area could be used to represent any place at will.

We shall now focus our attention solely upon the English Miracle plays and try to assess something of their impact upon a contemporary English audience.

Although cycles of Miracle plays are known to have been performed in many places throughout the British Isles, only five have been preserved in a condition that even approaches completeness. These are: the Chester; the York; and the Wakefield (Towneley) cycles; the so-called Coventry *Corpus Christi* Play which, because it seems not to have any connection at all with the city of Coventry, is commonly known as the 'N' Town Cycle; and the Cornish plays which were originally written in Cornish but partly translated into English during the seventeenth century. We also have a considerable part of the cycle which was performed by the Craft Guilds of Coventry; two versions of a play performed by the Grocers of Norwich; and the fragment of a play of Noah's Ark which belonged to the Shipwrights of Newcastle upon Tyne.

Of these cycles, those of Chester, York, Wakefield and Coventry were performed by craft guilds as, evidently, were the plays of Norwich and Newcastle. The 'N' Town Cycle, concerning which there is a great deal of mystery and speculation, is believed to have been performed, at least in its present state, by a company of clerics in a number of different towns: hence the name 'N' Town which is taken from a line in the banns of the cycle—which we should regard as an announcement of the performance to come, and which is assumed to allow for the actual name of the town to be announced as the case required. The Cornish plays, too, tend to stand apart as being of special character.

It is when we are thinking of the plays of the craft guilds that we begin to imagine the processional method of presentation. Here we are assisted in getting a fairly clear, though, it must be said, general idea of what took place, from the preserved records of the ancient craft guilds and city corporations. It has to be borne in mind, however, that each town or city made its arrangements independently according to its own traditions and practical requirements, so that we can never accept without proof that what was done, say, at Chester or Coventry, was necessarily done at York.

Each guild was responsible for the upkeep of its pageant and for the provision of actors from its own 'mystery' or craft. On rare occasions we are furnished with a little information concerning the pageants themselves. We hear from Chester, for example, of 'a highe place made like a howse with ii rowmes being open on ye top', the upper room providing the stage and the lower room providing a dressing room. Records of the Grocers' pageant at Norwich tell of a house with a square canopy built on four wheels. Doubtless, there would have been a considerable variation in the design of the pageants just as there is in the design of the floats in a modern carnival, and for reasons which are in many respects similar. Each pageant would have presented a magnificent spectacle, for we hear of richly gilded pennants surmounting the canopy and of the arms of the city and the guild responsible emblazoned upon its framework. We have to imagine the grandeur and generous sense of splendour and ancient civic pride when we think of a procession of mediaeval pageants being drawn through the streets of a town or city by bands of craftsmen and journey-men.

The illustration in Figure 7 shows a modern interpretation of a mediaeval pageant designed in 1952 by the artist Frederick Burgess for the Surrey Community Players. The play being performed

Fig. 7　A modern staging of the pageant play *The Creation*, from the Wakefield Cycle; lit by flambeaux for an evening performance in front of St Paul's Cathedral in London

is the Wakefield *Creation* which requires the three 'regions' of Heaven, Paradise and Hell. On the right of the upper platform the heavenly region is arranged on a slightly raised stage. Paradise with its tree is seen on the left, and behind it stands a cavern through which Lucifer and his rebellious angels can be hurled after their defeat. Hell with its dragon's mouth takes up the forward part of the lower stage, the rear part being used as a quick-changing room for the fallen angels who have to appear to the accompaniment of fireworks and belching smoke in a matter of seconds. When the play is over, the whole of the lower 'set' can be taken away so that the cast may sit, grouped in display, on their journey between one station and another.

The rules governing the rehearsal and performance of the craft cycles were strict. In York guilds were expected to provide 'good players, well arrayed and openly speaking', and an order from the same city, dated 3rd April 1476, calls for the appointment of 'four of the most cunning, discreet and able players within this city' to take upon themselves the task of examining the actors and inspecting the pageants to ensure that all should be done 'to the honour of the city and worship of the said crafts'.

Actors were paid according to the importance of their parts. The Drapers of Coventry paid three shillings and fourpence for 'the playing of God', for example, while at Hull one shilling was paid 'to Jenkin Smith for playing Noah'. Indiscipline among the actors was sternly checked, often, it seems, with the backing of a stiff fine, especially when it led to the forgetting or 'fluffing' of lines, frequently the result of heavy samplings of the liquor that was carried on board the pageants.

The clearest description of the way in which a cycle was managed comes from Chester. The description is late (early-seventeenth-century) but it speaks confidently of a tradition that had lasted for nearly three hundred years. In Chester, we are told, the plays were performed, not during the feast of Corpus Christi (as they were at York, Wakefield and Coventry) but on the Monday, Tuesday and Wednesday of Whitsun Week. On St George's Day a man 'fitted for ye purpose' rode through the city, 'and there published the tyme and the matter of ye plays in briefe, which was called ye reading of the banes' [banns].

The proclamation or reading of the banns by a herald on an appointed day before the performance of the cycles seems to have been common wherever they were performed: and it seems always to have been done with considerable ceremony. It was a sign, more often than not, of municipal authority, for besides announcing the time and content of the plays—which most of the people would have known already—the proclamation usually included a stern warning against any breach of the peace upon the day or days appointed for the performance. The carrying of offensive weapons was forbidden and any act of violence severely punished.

The Chester record goes on to describe how the plays were performed: one after the other, first at the Abbey gates, then before the Mayor and Corporation at the High Cross before passing on to Watergate Street and Bridge Street, and so on. In this way an audience could, if it wished, remain at one station and see all the plays performed there.

At York the performance of the plays was completed in one day. The players were ordered to assemble with their pageants 'at the mydhowre betwix iiijth and vth of the cloke in the mornynge', and then proceed in procession to their stations without waste of time. There seems to have been fierce competition amongst the citizens of York for the right to have the stations established opposite their houses, a privilege for which a fee was paid to the civic authority. It is when we consider arrangements like these that we can begin to appreciate the popularity of the cycles themselves and the excitement which they and the spectacle which they presented generated amongst the people. It is hardly surprising, therefore, when we learn that in time the pageants at York succeeded in ousting the Corpus Christi procession (in itself an impressive spectacle) which was moved to the following day.

Something has already been said in an earlier chapter about the quality of true popularity. Here we have to take due note of the socially saturating nature of this quality when applied to mediaeval theatre. For savage, oppressive and cruel though the age was in many respects, its appreciation of its theatre was almost completely classless. Many things are on record to support this view. It is known, for example, that in 1409 Henry IV with his court attended Miracle plays at Skinners' Well (Clerkenwell). At Coventry in 1457 Queen Margaret attended the plays and was given lodging by a certain Richard Woods, a grocer; while we learn that in 1397 Richard II attended the plays in York. A record which reflects the state of affairs at the other end of the social scale tells us that the common people were put to so much expense with their plays and pageants that they 'fared the worse' for the rest of the year. This was very likely the case, since we know that certain of the poorer guilds were so impoverished by the maintenance of their plays and pageants that they were forced to retire. All this, however, adds up to a general impression of the Miracle plays as a great annual event in the lives of rich and poor alike. The reader who wishes to extend his knowledge of the records relating to the presentation of mediaeval plays should consult E. K. Chambers's *The Mediaeval Stage*, Volume II, Appendix W, from which many of the citations in this chapter have been taken.

THE THEATRE OF
THE PEOPLE (CONT.)

II. THE MIRACLE PLAYS

And now, what of the Miracle plays themselves? What kind of dramatic spirit do they reflect, and what do they reveal about the general character of their mediaeval audiences? Obviously my treatment of the subject in this book must be brief. I shall nevertheless try to indicate the varied nature of the entertainment offered by dipping first into one cycle of plays and then into another, more or less at random. First of all, however, a word about the cycles as we have come to know them, and their probable dates.

Not one of the cycles exists in its original form. Each of the collections has been subjected to amendments and additions which reflect the work of a number of different authors, all of whom, with one possible exception, are anonymous. What little evidence of authorship exists points, not surprisingly, to men in holy orders, most probably monks. All the cycles bear distinct traces of the short liturgical dramas upon which most of the plays are based, many of them retaining here and there a few lines of the original Latin. As we might expect from collections of plays which have been written, improved and altered by so many hands, the overall effect is one of great variety, with sharp contrasts both in style and dramatic intensity which are at times quite startling. There are plays which, for us, make dull reading and still duller acting, while others enliven our imaginations into a vivid sense of robust mediaeval life and manners.

Scholars tend to differ in their opinions when it comes to the dating of particular cycles. This is not a matter of great concern to us in the present book, though we shall be sufficiently close to the truth if we accept the period from about 1325 to 1425 as the period of major strength in the history of the Craft Cycles in Britain. They continued to flourish during the fifteenth century but began to decline in the course of the sixteenth when they gradually lost their importance, partly as a result of the Reformation, but also because of the new ideas associated with the Renaissance.

As soon as we come to consider the plays in performance the question of approach arises. And here we need to turn our minds for a moment to certain peculiarities in the mediaeval interpretation of history, since, as we have already frequently emphasized, Christian legend was simple, factual history to the mediaeval mind.

Now, mediaeval people had a way of thinking about history which was vastly different from what we are used to. This does not mean that their way was inferior to our own: in fact it was in many ways advantageous, particularly when it came to presenting historical figures upon the stage. But what I have described as the acceptiveness of their minds seems to have gone hand in hand with a failure to regard time itself as a 'value', which to a modern historian would simply mean that they had no historical sense. For we *are* apt to regard time as a 'value' implying change or, to put it another way, our reading of history tends to give us a sense of 'period' and antiquity. The mediaeval view of history was quite different, for it showed little understanding of change in relation to time, although during the fourteenth century there were signs that the modern concept of history was beginning to dawn.

What this peculiarity meant in terms of the theatrical presentation of historical events is very important indeed because it accounts for a great deal of the colourfulness, sense of reality, and robust vitality which are to be found in the Miracle plays, especially in actual performance. Let us look at the matter in this way. If people are unable to regard change as an inevitable result of the passage of time, they naturally become inclined to regard people of past ages in exactly the same light as they regard themselves: and this is precisely what mediaeval dramatists seem to have done. To them, a carpenter living fourteen hundred years before their time was exactly the same in all his outward characteristics as a mediaeval carpenter. Similarly, a high priest living in Jerusalem at the time of Christ's crucifixion would be conceived at once as a mediaeval bishop. In other words, no matter whether they were thinking of an Old Testament prophet, a group of shepherds at the time of Christ's birth, or a woman of loose morals befriended by Christ during the period of his preaching, all were vividly imagined as mediaeval people.

The same sort of interpretation was at work in the mounting and costuming of their plays. A glance at the 'Doom' from the Holkham

Picture Bible shown in Plate 7 will provide evidence of this, for the characteristic was as common to the purely graphic as it was to the theatrical arts. The entrance to Heaven which appears at the lower left-hand side of the picture is a mediaeval tower-gateway, while the condemned king shown in the top right-hand section wears a mediaeval crown. Similarly, as a matter of course, Bethlehem, Nazareth and Jerusalem would have been conceived as walled cities built and embattled in a completely mediaeval fashion.

The significance of this 'timeless' conception of history lies in the fact that the legendary figures of the past become the living characters of the mediaeval present. Let us see what this means in terms of dramatic interpretation and theatrical impact.

I have already drawn attention to the figure or 'character' of God as he appears in the Chester *Deluge*. He is an angry, destructive figure who, as was suggested earlier, might easily retain the traces of pagan terror. Viewed simply as a stage 'character', however, he might conceivably strike a modern audience as a ranting bully bent on destroying the thing of his creation in a fit of rage. This would be a simplified view, but with a strong element of truth lying behind it. Let us see how this characterization of God might have struck a mediaeval audience.

The Flood was regarded in mediaeval times, not only as a very real event in history, but as one of the greatest possible significance. For it represented the end of the First World as originally created by God and destroyed by him because of the crimes of mankind. Nor do mediaeval people seem to have been in very much doubt as to the nature of these crimes. We know that a favourite book among the literate people of the fourteenth century was a narrative poem which was written in English and which set down the history of the world as it was then understood. This world history, which was given the Latin name of *Cursor Mundi*, has been preserved for us, and it tells us in frank terms what these unforgivable crimes were. We learn of men and women given over entirely to sensuality: of wives freely exchanged between husbands: and of people of both sexes indulging in homosexual practices:

> Ever they gave their lives to lust,
> That rotted their souls all to dust.
> Women, as we discover,

Went together against nature,
And men also the same way
As the devil would devise.

If the words of the *Cursor Mundi* reflect the popular mediaeval interpretation of the Flood legend, then we can at least get a glimpse of the significance of this particular figure of God to them. Here was the Avenging God cleansing his creation of corruption, and performing the task with cruel ruthlessness. But this is not the only aspect of the matter.

There is in the characterization of God in the Chester *Deluge* more than a touch of the mediaeval despot: the type of authority which in the knowledge of its brute strength tramples upon the weak whenever it is angrily disposed, and is at peace with the world as soon as it has got what it wants and its anger is spent. This, in theatrical terms, was a 'type' with which mediaeval people lived on terms of daily familiarity, and we find that it frequently appears in the Miracle cycles as a caricature of earthly as well as divine authority, sometimes to be 'guyed' as it frequently is in the character of the brutal King Herod.

Here, then, we get a complete transference of legendary matter from the past into the immediate experience of the present, and it is this characteristic probably more than any other that gives to mediaeval drama its vivid appeal and power of impact. Nor is the characteristic confined to the serious parts of the Miracle plays, for it is equally apparent in moments of farce. For example, the passages of sheer knockabout comedy that occur in the Chester *Deluge* simply feature a domestic situation between an aged and testy husband and a shrewish wife which was as amusing to a mediaeval audience as it is to a modern one. When Noah urges his wife to enter the ark, she obstinately refuses, almost as a matter of habit:

Noah
Good wife, do as I thee bid.

Wife
By Christ! not unless I see more need.
Though you stand all day and rave.

Noah
Lord, that women be crabbed aye,

And never are meek, that I dare say,
This is well seen of me today,
In witness of you each one. *(Pointing to the audience ——)*

Nobody cares that Noah's wife should swear by Christ long before the time of his nativity. The oath is accepted as a normal expression of mediaeval vehemence completely in character with a sharp-tongued woman of the time. It was common enough to depict Noah as something of an old fool, nagged and abused by a contemptuous and sceptical wife (in the Wakefield version, blows are exchanged between the two with a will) and, doubtless, mediaeval audiences looked forward to the moments of domestic conflict with relish. One should always remember, however, the additional edge imparted to such scenes by the mediaeval prejudice against women. The mediaeval male was constantly reminded that women were not merely 'crabbed' but were the evil descendants of the temptress Eve. The wood-carving shown in Plate 4B illustrates this point. Here we see a woman whose fine head-dress attracts the attentions of the two young gallants on either side, both being oblivious to the evil nature revealed in her countenance. It is most probable that the carving was inspired by a sermon warning young men against the wiles of women, and the carver seems to have derived a great deal of fun from the subject. This seems to have been a habit of the mediaeval mind and it is always interesting to look out for traces of it in the Miracle plays.

The swift changes between the farcical and the tragic in mediaeval drama are sometimes puzzling to the modern student, particularly when they appear in the short plays of the Miracle cycles. Certainly such changes might seem perverse, artless and wholly without a sense of dramatic propriety. So they might be; but it is surprising how much of what may look like the result of a 'hit and miss' approach, or an idle piece of fun-making on the part of the dramatist, succeeds in hitting very hard when seen in action upon the stage. The Chester *Deluge* offers an instance of this in the last farcical sequence of the play when Noah's wife is dragged from her drinking companions and carried forcibly to the ark by her sons, and, on arrival, rewards Noah with a resounding box on the ear. This is one of the many cases in which the modern producer, not knowing precisely what the author's intentions were, must make his individual judgement as to the potentials offered by the text. The producer who focuses the attention of the audience upon the 'gossips' by engaging them in the 'business' of a wailing, receding chorus as the rains commence, succeeds in achieving the impact of appalling tragedy as the voices fade, and the ark closes while the world drowns. In a moment like this the laughter evoked by farce can leave a powerfully mocking echo in the minds of an audience.

The natural desire in ourselves to analyse and speculate should never, of course, be allowed to stand in the way of our vision of mediaeval audiences simply as they were, which means that we have to accept them as people who loved the raw belly laughter of 'making sport', as they would have expressed it. We can, however, frequently find a point of some gravity behind the explosion: perhaps a matter of Christian doctrine too often dinned into their ears; or perhaps the burst of mockery that sometimes arises when power becomes oppressive or the hanger-on profits by becoming subservient to it. Even Noah might have appealed to the mediaeval fancy as God's special 'creep'. We shall never know.

One example of 'making sport' with a serious theme which calls for particular attention is to be found in the 'N' Town play of *The Woman Taken in Adultery*. The theme is one of deep human gravity and pathos, and it involves a number of subtleties.

A Scribe and a Pharisee plot together to discredit Jesus by trapping him into a denial of the Laws of Moses. They learn from an informer of an adulteress who at that very time of day lies in expectation of her lover. This provides the chance that the Scribe and the Pharisee have been hoping for. Knowing that Jesus preaches a new law of love and mercy, and knowing that according to the sacred law of the Jews an adulteress caught in the act must be stoned to death, they plan to seize the woman, drag her into the presence of Jesus and challenge him to decide what should be done to her.

Duly the Scribe, the Pharisee and the informer burst in upon the woman and her lover: and it is at this point that the belly laughter is evoked. For the lover is caught literally with his trousers down, and all is hubbub as he strives to threaten the intruders with a dagger and at the same time hoist his trousers to restore his mobility. Here is a case of 'making sport' with a quaint sense of stage economy. For the presence of the lover is obviously necessary, though once discovered he is immediately redundant; and to get rid of him in the midst of farcical uproar seems as good a way as any. But it is the sudden switch to intensely realistic tragedy that is particularly worthy of our study since it offers a perfect example of controlled tension (conflict) and release (catharsis).

The cries of the adulteress are piteous as she realizes that it is the firm purpose of her captors to have her stoned to death according to the letter of the Mosaic Law. The awareness in the audience that the foul abuse poured by the men upon their victim is cynically hypocritical serves to increase the theatrical tension: and this in turn enhances the effect of the climax and point of release.

The woman is dragged before Jesus who is addressed by the Scribe and the Pharisee in flattering terms as a 'wise prophet'. Then the trap is set for him:

> Of your conscience tell us plainly
> With this woman what shall be done.
> Shall we let her go in peace again
> Or to her death shall she be brought?

The part written for Jesus here is a masterpiece of dramatic control. He does not answer but slowly turns and begins to write in the sand at his feet while the woman falls to her knees and pleads with him for mercy. With sadistic irony the plotters urge Jesus to deliver his opinion quickly, but he continues silently and thoughtfully to write in the sand. When he does speak it is to call the attention of the conspirators to what he has written. Each man finds himself confronted with a record of his crimes, and each is overcome with confusion. Afraid of injury to their wretched reputations they slink away, leaving the woman with Jesus and their cunning question unanswered. As the Pharisee puts the case:

> If my fellows that do see
> They will tell it both far and wide.

Here surely enough is a case of 'the biter bit' and dramatized in complete harmony with the writer's experience of the people and manners of his own time. It would be difficult indeed to find a clearer example of an ancient legend so dramatically contrived that it becomes transformed into a perfect piece of contemporary entertainment.

But it is not always that the theatrical effectiveness of a Miracle play is so obvious: in fact, there are some plays which might easily fill the reader with wonderment at the apparent absurdity of their conception. The plays dealing with the Creation of the World and the Fall of Man are among these. Let us consider the Wakefield *Creation* as an example. Here we are confronted with an astonishing series of cosmic events crammed into a play which takes no more than thirty-five minutes to perform. During this time, God creates the world, the sun, the moon and the stars; he is worshipped by the company of angels in Heaven; Lucifer in his pride tries to usurp God's authority; war takes place in Heaven and Lucifer together with his rebellious followers is cast into Hell; God creates Man to take the place of Lucifer in his affections; and Lucifer, now Satan, plots with his companions to bring about the downfall of Man (the end of the play is lost). All this is performed within the limited space of a single pageant, possibly with the use of the street immediately below by Satan and his company of devils. But strangely enough it all works, as anyone who has seen a performance of this play on a pageant will readily testify.

By saying that the play works we mean, of course, that it succeeds in creating a complete stage illusion in which its audience becomes completely absorbed. The reasons why this is so could involve us in a great deal of discussion for which there is insufficient space, but it may be helpful to emphasize one or two points which have a direct bearing on what has so far been said.

The conflicts involved in the play are bold, sharp, simple, and, which is probably the most important point of all, based solidly upon the sort of behaviour that mediaeval audiences could readily appreciate. God in the Wakefield *Creation* is a sublime figure, for reasons that we shall offer in a moment. The disastrous ambitions of Lucifer are, however, frankly human. He first betrays his pride when God is off the stage—behind God's back, as it were. He swells with self-admiration, seats himself upon God's throne and shows off before the rest of the angels. He is, he says, brighter than the sun and quite the equal of God. Do not the rest of the angels agree with him?

> Say, felows, how semys now me
> To sit in seyte of trinyte?
> I am so bright of ich a lym*   [*in every limb]
> I trow me seme as well as hym.

It is all so completely human, even in its immaturity. Thus, we might imagine, would a young modern office employee behave on entering an unoccupied board-room in a fit of curiosity, surrounded by a group of his fellows. The seat of the Chairman acts as an irresistible magnet, and he shows off to his grinning companions: until the Chairman of the Board makes a sudden unexpected entry. The situation in the case of Lucifer is not dissimilar, except that what it represents is not a joke. But because it reflected for its mediaeval audience the sheer mischief, or even prankishness, of pride in honestly human terms it could be stated briefly, dramatically, and convincingly.

As always when we are dealing with the Miracle cycles, we have to adjust ourselves, as far as we are able, to certain mediaeval interpretations of the Christian legend. Otherwise, things are likely to go awry when we come to produce them on stages of our own. There are two such points of interpretation which appear in all the plays concerned with the Creation and the Fall of Man. The first of these lies in the characterization of God himself. For God the Creator is vastly different from God the Destroyer as seen in all the plays concerned with the Flood. In creation God is sublime: the ultimate Principle who has no beginning and no ending, and whose very thought *is* creation. In the Wakefield version God announces himself in words like these:

> *Ego sum alpha et o,*
> I am the first, the last also,
> One god in majesty . . .
>
> I am without beginning,
> My godhood has no ending . . .
>
> All things are in my thought,
> Without me there may be nought. . . .

This is the mediaeval conception of the God who created Man originally in his own image and a far cry from the 'God' created by fallen Man in the image of himself. To mediaeval people, at least, the distinction seems to have been important.

The next point concerns the eating of the Forbidden Fruit by

Adam and Eve which symbolized the Fall of Man. To mediaeval people the eating of the fruit of the Tree of Knowledge of Good and Evil (oddly enough the Wakefield play confuses it with the Tree of Life) symbolized the 'original sin' of usurping the knowledge and power which were the sole prerogative of the ultimate authority, God. This is a problem with which thinking people are not un-acquainted today, though the thinking takes place against a totally different background and not necessarily with reference to God. Whatever differences exist, however, we have to be careful to give due weight to the importance of the symbol in the minds of a mediaeval audience. This is not to suggest, of course, that mediaeval audiences, flushed with festival gaiety and excitement, cared to reflect, or were even capable of reflecting, upon universal problems. It is important to remember, nevertheless, that their minds were vividly orientated towards a consciousness of sin and its origins. This is a matter which will claim our close attention in the next chapter.

Each of the complete cycles presents the killing of Abel immediately after the Fall of Man. Here we get the committing of the first murder as a reflection of Man in a 'state of sin'. Cain murders his younger brother Abel because he is jealous of him and because his pride is offended. Abel is a good man who prospers and finds favour in the eyes of God because he accepts the burden of labour that God has now placed upon mankind. Cain, on the other hand, is a rebel who sees no reason for offering his tenth or 'tithe' to God. Why should he? After all, as he says in the 'N' Town version, God does no work.

Now, here was a theme which introduced a bone of contention dear to the hearts of many mediaeval people. For it concerned the duty of offering one-tenth of their incomes, either in kind or in money, to God; which in practical terms meant the Church. The paying of 'tithe' was a great burden to many and a cause of grievance to most, so that the clergy were frequently moved to remind their congregations from the eminence of the pulpit of what their duties were, and why. Obviously the story of Cain and Abel was the right lesson to choose, with the result that the Old Testament legend probably ranked among the most thoroughly preached themes in mediaeval times. Much of the treatment of the theme in the Miracle plays reflects the popular reaction to this irksome cause of contention between Church and people, and it is partly for this reason, most probably, that the character of Cain the murderer is usually to be found more interesting and, in a theatrical sense, more entertaining than the character of his brother. To this, of course, we need to add that throughout the history of popular theatre the criminal has most frequently proved more interesting than his victim.

All these points are most clearly represented in the Wakefield play of *The Killing of Abel*, in which the characterization of Cain is exceptionally powerful. He appears as a coarse-tongued, oafish brute with a permanent sense of grievance against all and sundry, and against God in particular. As a mediaeval 'type' he represents the labouring farmer whose constant lack of success has produced a permanent chip on his shoulder. Like most people with a persistent sense of failure and deprivation, he treats all people alike with defiance and rudeness. His chief delight, however, is to be defiantly rude in his references to God. When it comes to his turn to make his sacrifice he plays the clown and juggles with his sheaves of corn, reserving the best for himself, and selecting the meanest and barest for his offering. When Abel stoutly protests against this obvious piece of trickery, Cain reacts with the rude defiance that the audience has now come to expect from him. God shall have not one bit more:

> Not so much, great nor small,
> As he might wipe his arse withal.

When Cain sets fire to his meagre sacrifice it merely smoulders, smothering him with stinking smoke that sends him choking and cursing into retreat. Incensed by this insult to his pride he turns the full force of his anger upon his brother until God appears above to reprove him. Cain, however, is not impressed. Jerking his head in the direction of the figure of God, he shouts to Abel:

> Why, who is that hob-over-the-wall?
> Whe! who was that who piped so small?

It would be interesting to know, were it possible, how mediaeval audiences reacted to this scene. At a guess it seems probable that a few grave souls would have shaken their heads, though it would have been exquisite joy to most.

When Abel turns to leave his brother in disgust, the latter stops him. Cain has a score to settle first, he says. He accuses Abel of having stolen the favour of God, and when his brother tries to reason with him he brutally slays him. And here we note a certain consistency in the characterization of Cain that is well worth our special attention. For instead of revealing the remorse and terror which are displayed in varying degrees by other portrayals of Cain in the Miracle plays, he remains obstinately defiant. When he has killed his brother he turns to the audience and dares them to blame him. If they do, he says, he will soon make matters worse. When God calls him to account he still shows no remorse:

> Since I have done so great a sin
> That I may not thy mercy win,
> And thou thus thrust me from thy grace,
> I shall hide me from thy face.

Which, surely, is the defiance of despair, which is not without its element of pathos.

It seems clear that what we are given in this characterization of Cain is something more than a reflection of rebellion and the violent consequences of jealous hatred. It is a vivid, penetrating portrait of a mediaeval churl; ignorant; brutal and utterly blind to reason; a coarse and savage clown; though capable, because he is so human, of being pitied. Such a portrait demands the hand of a master dramatist, and it is more than likely that we have in the Wakefield *Killing of Abel* a play written by the dramatist known as the Wakefield Master, an author whose contributions to the Wakefield cycle are marked by a wry, sometimes bitter wit, and a penetrating satirical sense that is frequently relieved by a contrasting sense of pathos.

When we come to the plays which deal with the great climactic points of the Christian legend, namely, the Birth of Jesus, his Passion, Execution and Resurrection, we get the same feeling of a living theatre projected from a sacred theme. And here, perhaps, we are given genuine reason for surprise. For in our own age we have grown accustomed to a certain degree of idealization in the portrayal of such figures as the Virgin Mary, Joseph her husband, Christ's disciples and, of course, Jesus himself. But in the Miracle plays there is no such thing. We find that all the personalities presented on the stage are 'real' rather than idealistic because they emerge so honestly from their mediaeval background. Mary the mother of Jesus, for example, is as much a woman of her own time as is Noah's wife, while Joseph her husband offers a very convincing image of a fourteenth-century carpenter. The overall effect from a dramatic and theatrical point of view can be excitingly intimate as no modern portraiture of these figures could be. We shall be able to consider no more than a few examples to illustrate this point, but let us try to make them as suitable to our purpose as we can. First of all let us take the situation between Joseph and Mary when the latter is in a state of pregnancy.

According to the legend (St Matthew, Chapter 1) 'before they came together' Mary was 'found with child of the Holy Ghost'. Because her husband had never been to bed with her he suspected the obvious cause of his wife's pregnancy but 'being a just man and not willing to make her a public example (he) was minded to put her away privily'. This circumstance as dramatized in the Miracle cycles became known as *Joseph's Trouble* which is depicted in every play as a quarrel or 'stress' between an aged and impotent husband who believes himself to have been betrayed and bamboozled in every possible way, and a young wife who has certain knowledge of her innocence. A more lifelike and honestly conceived situation could hardly be imagined, and it is theatrically presented in a full-blooded and on occasions in a brutally realistic way.

Plate 6, which is taken from the Holkham Picture Book Bible, pictures the scene as it might easily have taken place on the mediaeval stage. Joseph in his anger is in the act of grasping his wife around the abdomen as he demands to know how she became pregnant. Let us take the scene from that point as it is dramatized in the Wakefield version.

Joseph
Who owe this child thou   [*Who gave you this child?*]
  gose with all?

Mary
Sir, ye, and god of heven.   [*Sir, you and God in heaven.*]

(*Here we may suppose that Joseph moves in to strike her.*)

Joseph
Myne, mary? do way thi dyn;   [*Mine, Mary?*
                                 Give me none of that!
That I shuld oght have   *You know that I could have had*
  parte therin   *No part in it.*]
Thou nedys it not to neven.

The scene builds up in intensity as Joseph accuses and Mary maintains her innocence. But it becomes apparent that what Joseph really yearns for is the restoration of his pride which has been injured by his wife in making a fool of him. He will be understanding and make allowances for the reckless desires of her youth if only she will confess the truth:

> *Joseph*
> I blame the not, so god me save,
> Woman maners* if that thou have,   [*woman's ways]
>   Bot certys* I say the this,   [*But certainly]
> Well wote* thou, and so do I,   [*know]
> Thi body fames the openly,
>   That thou has done amys*.   [*amiss]

Mary's reply as she departs from the scene is that of a wife, sure of her good faith, but in despair of being believed:

> *Mary*
> Yea, god, he knowys all my doyng.

So here again we get a scene, this time a not uncommon domestic one, particularly as it takes place between an aged husband and a young wife, that is completely convincing because it is rooted in the everyday experience of the audience for which it was written. And here we might be tempted to carry the point a little bit further than we have done up to now.

The scene that we have just quoted, if considered simply as a domestic situation and apart from its particular legend, is just as capable of appealing to a modern theatre audience as it was to the people of Wakefield when it was performed there. This is because it reflects so accurately the thoughts, emotions and reactions of two people involved in one particular kind of stress. A modern audience would accept as readily as its mediaeval counterpart that an aged and impotent husband finding his young wife pregnant might well be deeply wounded in his pride, in which case he would do precisely as Joseph does and, perhaps violently, try to wring the truth from her. On the other hand, a young wife who has reason to be convinced of her good faith and who has nothing to explain, always supposing this to be possible, would suffer the stress just as Mary suffers it. In other words, so recognizably human are Joseph and Mary in this particular situation that they break down the barriers of time and represent man and wife in a similar situation everywhere and at any time. When a play does this we say that its theatrical appeal is universal, which is about the highest praise we can give it. There are many plays, and sometimes scenes, in the Miracle cycles which strike us with the same quality. The scene which I have already quoted from *The Woman Taken in Adultery* has it, for instance. Such cases are always worthy of the closest study on the part of the appreciative student, especially if he or she is a keen student of the theatre of Shakespeare, with whose work 'universality of appeal' is always most closely associated. It is good to note how the quality began to flourish when the dramatic art itself was still in its cruder stages.

It is the same frank honesty of approach that makes the Passion plays so convincing, even when they are shocking in their wanton savagery, as they frequently are. In the York cycle, for example, there are scenes of brutality which are all too clearly mediaeval in their nature. It was the common practice of the age to make a scourging, whether administered to a criminal or not, as deliberately insulting as it was sadistically cruel. These were the familiar characteristics of the age in which the man Jesus appears on the popular stage, suffering the butchery inflicted on him with the deep tragic eloquence of silence. Thus, strictly within the context of their own times, were mediaeval audiences able to 'behold the Man'. For the Jesus of the Miracle plays is most supremely a man, and it is through the absoluteness of his manhood that his divinity is made dramatically apparent.

The same thought can arise, though I am not suggesting that it necessarily does so, when in the York *Crucifixion* Christ is nailed to the cross. Here the torturers joke coarsely with one another as they stretch the limbs of their victim to reach the auger holes which have been placed too far apart. Torturers in mediaeval times did exult over their victims and they did make coarse jokes at their expense.

I have one further example to introduce, which is a short passage from the York cycle in which Christ is appearing for trial before Pilate. In this scene there is a sharp clash of characters as Pilate shows his contempt for Christ's chief accusers, Caiaphas and Annas. The last two, because in the legend they were high priests, would have appeared in the garb of mediaeval bishops, and, whether by design or not, they fit perfectly into the characters of mediaeval bishops of the worst kind: politically cunning, fawning, and ever ready to bend ecclesiastical law to the furtherance of their personal power and influence. The scene, which has been modernized, comes from the York play of the Tapestry Makers.

As Jesus is brought into the court the Beadle (or court usher) bows before him. This action is immediately challenged by Annas and Caiaphas, and the Beadle simply explains with what reverence Jesus has been greeted by the people on his entry into Jerusalem. Caiaphas accuses the Beadle of twisting the truth, but the latter stoutly denies this. Then Annas rises to his feet with the object of shouting the Beadle down:

Annas
I say hold your tongue, you hireling,
and stop speaking contrary to your betters.

Pilate (to Annas)
When you have finished your bickering, I shall begin my examination.

Annas
Sir, doom him [*Jesus*] to death. Do away with him.

Pilate
Sir, have you done?

Annas
Yes, my lord.

Pilate
Then sit down and be quiet,
and leave it to me to decide what is lawful.

I have introduced this scene for two reasons. In the first place, it is a passage which might well appeal to any modern actor, particularly if he is cast in the role of Pilate, while, in the second place, it should be fairly obvious that the theatrical impact must depend upon the quality of the acting and the control of stage delivery. For there seems little doubt that we should most of us agree that the theatrical and dramatic potentials of the scene are great. First we have the Beadle's explanation of his respectful treatment of Jesus. This involves a notable piece of dramatic economy because the author uses the Beadle to inject into the consciousness of his audience the exciting event of Christ's triumphant entry into Jerusalem which is really the background of his present scene. Then there is the bullying speech of Annas as he tries to shout the Beadle down, using the authority of his priestly rank in the process. Immediately following we have the calm, incisive authority of the law represented by Pilate who, with thinly veiled contempt, pricks the balloon of hatred and prejudice generated by the two high priests. Finally we have the silent, dignified figure of Jesus standing between his guards, already aware of what his fate will be.

What did the mediaeval actors make of all this potential? Did they deliver the scene with all the dignity that tragic playing demands? Were they sufficiently trained in enunciation to impart to their lines the resonance of anger and the nuances of quiet, contemptuous authority that the scene called for? Was the actor who played the part of Jesus sufficiently a master of 'playing in repose' to reflect the divine nobility and humility of Christ as he is characterized in the play? Above all, were they capable of appreciating the skills required of them?

The answer to all these questions is that we do not really know. One thing that we do know, perhaps a little unfortunately in some respects, is that during the second half of the sixteenth century the ineptitude of players in the Miracle cycles had become a subject for humorous comment and half-embarrassed self-apology. But this was a time when the Miracle cycles had lost most of their significance and the main focus of the English stage was changing rapidly. The problem is a ticklish one, though we are not left entirely without guidance. We have already noted the attention given to the skills of acting by the priests who performed *Le Mystère d'Adam* as early as the twelfth century and by the craft guilds who performed the Miracle cycles of the fourteenth century. We know, too, to what extent the pride of the guilds was involved in the production of the Miracle plays when their importance and popularity were at their peak. When we couple this knowledge, scrappy and incomplete though it is, with what we know of the lavishness of expenditure in Britain and on the continent upon the stages and the overall trappings of the mediaeval theatre, it seems hardly likely that the actual performance of the plays would have been left to the fumbling efforts of the unskilled and inadequately rehearsed.

Finally, we have to turn to the evidence of the plays themselves. It is true that in terms of literary quality the plays vary considerably, not only from one cycle to another, but also from one play to another. But the general tendency seems to be to undervalue rather than overvalue the quality of many of the plays, among which there may be found passages of outstanding beauty and simplicity, and, which is even more important, aptness of dramatic expression. Nevertheless, when all this has been considered, the fact remains that the mediaeval theatre was above all things a theatre of the actor and producer. We have been able to consider no more than a few examples of scenes extracted from the Miracle plays. All the examples chosen, however, reveal a strength of dramatic and theatrical potential which it is not easy to ignore. It would be strange indeed if such passages had been written by authors who could see no way in which the potentials could be exploited.

6

RELIGION AND
THE STAGE

Up to the present I have used the word 'religion' as sparingly as possible. This is because, as I have already explained, our own meaning of the term would hardly be recognizable to a mediaeval person, no matter what the state of his education and learning. We must now, however, use the word, and in doing so, try to understand what it probably did mean to the average mediaeval man or woman. For the plays which we have to consider in this, the last chapter of our book, have religion for their subject, though one of them at least deals with its theme in a manner which falls a long way short of reverence.

A careful examination of the 'Doom' or Last Judgement illustrated in Plate 7 should help us on our way. The picture is typical of many of its kind which may be found in varying states of preservation painted upon the walls of mediaeval churches. Central to the picture is the figure of Christ who sits in judgement beneath a Gothic canopy. He displays the wounds of the Crucifixion which signify the divine act of Redemption. We are to suppose that his judgement of 'the living and the dead' has been given because with his right hand he beckons those whose souls have been saved while with his left he spurns the condemned who are being dragged away in chains by a hideous devil. Note that all the souls are naked and that they have been judged without respect to rank, status and calling, for a king, a bishop and three monks are shown amongst the damned.

The lower half of the picture shows the contrasting destinies of those who have been saved and those who have not. On the left the former are being welcomed within the portals of Heaven by two angels while the latter are shown on the right with attendant demons in the regions of Hell. Every detail shows the simple literalness of the mediaeval interpretation of things. Heaven is seen as a contemporary Gothic palace where love, peace and 'mirth' (indicated by music) reign for ever, while Hell is represented by a torture chamber set in what appears to be the dungeon of a castle. We have to remember this ready translation of abstract ideas into physically tangible realities because it is extremely important to us in this chapter.

As we try to imagine the impact of the 'Doom' upon the individual Christian of the time we have to bear in mind that for him it represented the final commitment in a timeless universe. Once the Last Judgement had been delivered there was no appeal. The soul, now re-united with an incorruptible body, faced its eternal destiny which was either one of perpetual joy, or one of unremitting, intolerable pain. This was a terrifying prospect and there can be no doubt that mediaeval people saw it in that way.

The prospect of the Last Judgement and its consequences placed a specially solemn emphasis upon the physical fact of death. Once the blow of the 'Awful Striker' had fallen, the soul's conflict was at an end and its ultimate fate depended upon the mercy of the Divine Judge. And here, once more, we have to dwell upon the grim physical realities of the age with its high death rate and its helplessness in the face of disease and the apparent whims of nature. In such conditions, it seems, mediaeval people were driven to two extremes, for on the one hand they reveal a zest for living and a love of colour and magnificence which the modern Western world might easily envy, while on the other hand they seem to have been weighed down by an obsessive horror of death.

Plate 8 shows how death was commonly imaged in the mediaeval mind. The painting shows Death, armed with a dagger, striking a cardinal. Note that the cardinal's facial expression betrays no suspicion of what is befalling him at that awful moment. With a remarkable subtlety of hand, the artist portrays him in the fullness of ecclesiastical pride and power, with very little positive expression apart from contented expectation that what has been will continue to be. So Death is symbolized as the secret striker who respects neither the time nor the person. He is the stealthy equalizer whose blow strips the victim of all power and wealth, reducing him to the nakedness which all men share, and ultimately to dust. Beyond that point of oblivion the only thing to remain was the ultimate and inevitable destruction of the world and the determination of the soul's destiny for the infinity of time.

This picture, taken from a painted panel at Hexham Abbey in Northumberland, is again typical of the symbolism of the time: and, like the 'Doom' painting, acted as a powerful reminder to the mediaeval conscience. And herein lay the point of religion so far as it affected the mind of the common man.

What was probably the most appalling and frightening thing about the human soul to the mediaeval mind was its essential loneliness. It was born into the world and given a body, and therefore senses. Once born it was subject to conflict—not conflict of its own making, but the eternal war between the powers of Heaven and Hell; light and darkness; in which the warring parties strove for the conquest of every individual soul. The strife was closely akin to a siege and, as we shall find, it *was* frequently imagined as a warlike siege and so depicted upon the stage.

Thus we can see that the main focal point of mediaeval Christianity lay with the salvation of the souls of men, which meant that, religiously speaking, every Christian pursued a lonely course through the life of this world, with his mind and soul under constant assault from the temptations of the flesh, for it was through his senses or physical appetites that he was most vulnerable to the Devil. There were certain men and women, monks, nuns and others, who chose to 'leave the world' and under vows of celibacy, obedience and poverty dedicate their lives to the salvation of their souls. Only such as these, who had devoted themselves to one form of religious discipline or another, were entitled to the name 'religious'. The rest relied for the most part upon the offices of priests and preaching friars to reach and maintain the 'state of Grace' necessary for salvation.

All this needs to be borne in mind by the student and reader who wishes to extract the maximum interest from the Morality play, and from plays which are closely allied to it. For in its purest form, the Morality play was written with the direct purpose of appealing through entertainment to the consciences of its audience. In other words, its purpose was instructive or, as we say, didactic. Many plays have been written in our own age with the same purpose in view, though their appeal has been directed to the social and philosophical rather than the spiritual consciences of their audience.

The Morality play, which seems to have risen quickly to popularity during the second half of the fourteenth century, evolved largely from the sermon. The mediaeval sermon could be, and frequently was, vividly and grippingly illustrated with symbolical examples in order to entertain and enliven the imaginations of the people. This, too, was the intention of the Morality play. Its themes involved argument (in itself a conflict) and it used its stage and its actors symbolically to demonstrate and personify ideas.

What is fundamental to our interest in the Morality play is its use of the lonely character beset by difficulties which are likely to overwhelm him. This is a theme which is as adaptable to the play as it is to the sermon. It is also one which seems to prove its popularity in any age among old and young alike. In the Morality play, however, the theme was adapted allegorically.

Now, just in case we are not quite sure what an allegory is, let us build up an everyday example for ourselves. We can do this by supposing that we see a drunken man in the streets. Our most probable reaction would be to register the thought, 'There goes a drunk.' But now suppose that we first set eyes on our drunk when we are walking in the company of a friend with whom we are discussing the folly of drinking too much. Then it is quite possible that, struck with the imbecile wanderings and obvious physical distress of the poor man, we should nod our head in his direction and say to our companion, 'There goes drunkenness.' In other words, we create an allegory by transposing a flesh-and-blood drunk into a symbol. Drunkenness is not flesh and blood: it is a quality and therefore an abstraction.

To the mediaeval conscience drunkenness was not a folly, but a sin, though, let it be quickly said, neither a serious nor an uncommon one. Nevertheless, it could be a symptom of a far greater sin, namely, the sin of Gluttony. This was a sin so deadly that it put the soul of anyone possessed by it in danger of damnation. There were seven of these 'Deadly Sins' to which the following names were given: Pride; Envy; Lust or Lechery; Wrath; Covetousness or Avarice; Gluttony; Sloth.

As a counterbalance to the Seven Deadly Sins there were the Seven Graces or Seven Virtues which always worked in support of the individual soul in its journey through life. These were: Meekness; Charity; Abstinence; Chastity; Industry; Generosity; Patience.

100

All these sins and virtues were abstract values capable of representation on the stage in flesh-and-blood terms. Set in opposition or conflict they could create a drama: and this is what the Morality play did.

The most elementary of the Morality plays to have come down to us is *The Castle of Perseverance* which was written during the first quarter of the fifteenth century. The play, which is exceedingly long, depicts the allegorical character of Mankind in his journey through life, giving an account of the evils that beset him and the virtues that work and fight for his protection.

The skeletal plot is simple and, on first reading at least, rather dull for such a long play. Mankind appears in his state of innocence escorted by two advisers: his Good Angel and his Bad Angel. On the advice of the latter he gives himself over to the World, the Flesh and the Devil, all of whom are represented as living characters. And in a worldly sense he prospers, living richly and sensuously. When he has grown old in sin and self-indulgence, Shrift comes upon him and calls him to repentance. Mankind hears the call, confesses his sins and is restored to a state of Divine Grace, after which he asks to be taken to a place where he can be protected against evil. He is conducted to the Castle of Perseverance where he is placed under the care of the Seven Virtues. Hearing of Mankind's repentance, Belial (Satan) leads his host in an attack upon the castle, but he is driven off by the Seven Virtues. Not to be beaten, Belial decides to tempt Mankind out of the castle by guile. He sends for Covetousness who persuades Mankind, ever vulnerable to riches, to desert the castle. Mankind is conducted to a bed where he rests while Covetousness goes to gather more wealth for him. At this point Death enters and strikes Mankind with his dart. Thus stricken, Mankind reproves his tempters by whose means he has been brought to the point of death with all his sins upon him, and he dies crying upon God for mercy.

The theme is now taken up by Mankind's soul who seeks the aid of Mercy. But Mankind's Bad Angel, declaring that Mankind's relapse into sin has earned his eternal damnation, carries the Soul on his back into Hell. There follows a debate between Mercy, Truth, Righteousness and Peace concerning the ultimate fate of Mankind. They are unable to agree since Mercy and Peace argue for leniency while the others are for judging Mankind according to his deserts. The four take the case to God who decides in favour of Mercy and Peace. The Soul of Mankind is delivered from torment and brought to Heaven.

So much for the bare bones of the plot or argument. We can now examine the play in the light of its theatrical and dramatic appeal. And here we are most fortunate because the original manuscript of the play is furnished with a plan which shows the complete layout of the *platea* or 'place' which formed the acting area. With this and the instructions given in the scenario we are able to form a reasonably accurate picture of the way in which the play was staged.

The plan is reproduced in Figure 8. It will be seen that the acting

Fig. 8   Plan for a performance of *The Castle of Perseverance*

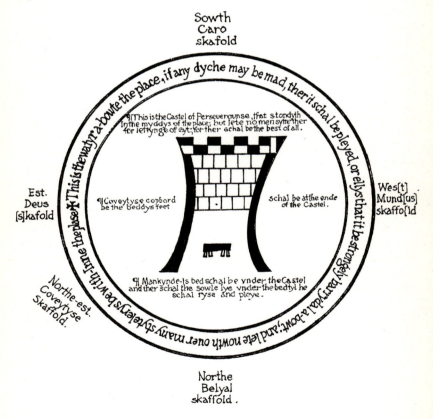

area is surrounded by a ditch for which could be substituted, whenever necessary, a fence or any other form of barrier. At the centre of the area which, according to the directions included in the plan, must be kept clear of spectators, is the castle. Below the wall of the castle is the bed upon which Mankind must lie when he is tempted out of the care of the Seven Virtues, and it is directed that the unfortunate player cast in the part of Mankind's Soul must lie beneath the bed 'tyl he schal ryse and pleye'.

Within the ditch at points indicated on the plan are the scaffolds or stages of God, Flesh, the World, Belial or Satan and Covetousness. We have to imagine each scaffold decorated in accordance with its subject. For example, Flesh announces in the play that he covers his towers with 'tapestries of taffeta' as a sign of lustful pleasure. The terrors of Satan are fortified by his having 'gunpowder burning in pipes in his hands and in his ears and in his arse when he goeth into battle'. It is also directed that the Four Daughters of God should be dressed in mantles of specific colours: 'Mercy in white; Righteousness in red, altogether [*entirely*]; Truth in sad [*sober*] green; and Peace all in black.' These colours were in themselves symbolical to the mediaeval mind.

What we have building up before us is a colourful composite picture which is very much like a series of wall paintings or stained glass windows brought to life. We need to take this into consideration when we are trying to assess the impact of the play upon its mediaeval audience. For we are dealing with an age which loved the bravery and sheer symbolism of colour, so that spectacle alone would have proved a very strong attraction.

As is the case with all mediaeval theatres of the fixed stage type, the action of the play moves from one scaffold or sub-stage to another as the plot requires. The pace is necessarily slow when judged by modern standards. This is largely because of the need to extend the dialogue sufficiently to point the moral and at the same time demonstrate the human psychological pattern associated with it. The student who cares to submit this particular feature of the *Castle of Perseverance* to close study should find himself well rewarded, for he will be able to see a certain development in the art of stage characterization which comes with the dawning in the playwright of a critical attitude to human behaviour. In other words, in this one important respect the *Castle of Perseverance* anticipates the 'break-through' in the dramatic and theatrical

103

art which was to become one of the great glories of the following century. There is insufficient space in the present book to explain this point in detail, but we can offer a few examples as a guide.

When Mankind makes his first entry into the arena he is escorted by his Good Angel and his Evil Angel and he declares himself as a newly born child:

> Wherefore I was to this world brought,
>> I know not; but to woe and weeping
> I am born, and have right nought
>> To help myself in no doing.

This at once touches off the allegorical theme, and as it does so it strives to arouse the sense of pity in its audience. Every man is born to live as a lonely, pitifully helpless creature. He has instincts for good and evil (his attendant angels) which govern his impulses in his journey through life. But he is beset all the while with temptations which are not of his making. Rather are they a part of Hell's plan to gain advantage in its perpetual war with the forces of Heaven. However this picture might appear to us, it certainly represents the way in which the average member of a mediaeval audience would have interpreted his own existence.

What follows after the appearance of Mankind is a perfect piece of allegory because the moral that it emphasizes is also clearly indicative of the trend of human nature. Mankind's Evil Angel, despite the vigorous protests of his Good Angel, persuades him to enjoy life and not worry about the salvation of his soul until he is sixty. Thus is Mankind laid open to the temptations of the World, and Folly steps in as the tempter:

> Come on, Man! Thou shalt not rue*   [*You will not be sorry]
>> If thou wilt be to us true,
> Thou shalt be clad in clothes new,
>> And be rich evermore.

Mankind says that he 'would [like to] be rich and of great renown' and is promptly whisked off by Folly and Lust to the scaffold of the World where he is dressed in rich garments and receives the promise of wealth and power. The moral would have been clear and dramatic enough to a mediaeval audience with the picture of the 'Doom' engraved upon its mind. Mankind is now open to the assaults of Covetousness and the most deadly sin of all: Pride. But the student of English Drama and Theatre might easily detect in the episode a strong sign of things to come. For the words and behaviour of Folly foreshadow the 'con' man of the Elizabethan stage, just as Mankind foreshadows his innocent 'gull'. The impression becomes even more substantial when Folly and Lust introduce Mankind to the World, their master:

Of worldly good is all his thought;
Of lust and folly he hath no schame;
   He would be gret* of name;   [*great]
He would be at gret honour
For to rewle* towne and toure*,   [*rule over] [*tower]
He wolde have to his paramoure*   [*as his mistress]
   Sum lovely dynge* dame.   [*high-born]

This reflects the sarcasm of the mediaeval allegory, and one can almost hear the biting words of the mediaeval preacher. Change the theatrical focus, however, to one of direct social satire and the words become those of the Elizabethan 'con' man mocking his victim while in the process of cheating him. When, a little later, it becomes the turn of Covetousness to instruct Mankind in the ways of the World, the acid voice of the reforming preacher merges even more with the tones of social satire:

Hear no beggar, though he cry —
And when thou useth merchandise*   [*whenever you trade]
Look that thou be subtle of sleight* [*cunning in dealing]
And also swear by deceit;
Buy and sell by false weight;
For that is natural covetise.

We are not very far away from the conscious art of stage character-ization here. But we shall have an opportunity to observe a further development in this direction before we close our chapter.

Interesting though these historical steps may be, however, one should not readily lose sight of the allegorical meaning of the *Castle of Perseverance*, nor cease in one's efforts to assess its theatrical impact upon the audience for whom the play was intended. This is a good point to bear in mind whenever we are considering the theatre of a past age. *The Castle of Perseverance* presented a spectacle of colourful imagery which must to a large extent be lost upon ourselves. We may appreciate this more, perhaps, by considering the main focal point of the play's action. This is the attack by Satan and his hordes upon the Castle and its defence by the Seven Heavenly Virtues. According to the play directions, the bellicose Satan with fire pouring from every conceivable orifice is completely beaten when he is pelted with roses. Even when we learn that in mediaeval times roses were the emblem of Christ's Passion, it is difficult, if not impossible, to feel the impact of the action quite as a mediaeval audience would have felt it. So must it be to a very great extent with the whole of this remarkable play.

We have now to consider what is by common consent the greatest Morality play known to us. This is the play of *Everyman* which is an allegory of Death and the preparation of mankind for the dreaded 'Moment of Reckoning'.

In dealing with its solemn subject the allegory of *Everyman* reflects the psychology of its times even more vividly than the *Castle of Perseverance*. With the exception of Death and Good Deeds, all the figures or characters in the play are closely linked to the pleasures, memories and even the five senses of a typical man, so that the play may be seen as a speculation or solemn reflection upon the disintegration of human consciousness at the onset of death. So intense is the 'message' implied by these symbolical figures and their falling away one by one from the doomed Everyman that the common reaction, even amongst a modern audience, is a curious mixture of horror and pathos.

The action of the play is perfectly simple. God, angry that mankind should have become so engrossed in the amassing of wealth that he and the need for his mercy are forgotten, sends for his messenger, Death, whom he dispatches to Everyman (note the connection with the painting shown in Plate 8) with the following words:

> And shew him, in my name,
> A pilgrimage he must on him take,
> Which he in nowise may escape;
> And that he bring with him a sure reckoning,
> Without delay or any tarrying.

Everyman is then seen walking in the distance, and Death, lying in wait, suddenly confronts him:

> Everyman, stand still! Whither art thou going
> Thus gaily? Hast thou thy maker forgotten?

Everyman is told that he is now required by God to make reckoning and that he must be ready to depart on a long journey at the end of which he must render up his account. In vain does Everyman plead for respite. Death is not to be put off by riches nor by pope, emperor, king, duke nor prince. On Everyman's asking if he may return once he has completed his journey, he is told that there is no return, though he may if he can find anyone who is sufficiently willing and courageous, take him as a companion.

Upon the departure of Death the allegory begins to open out. Everyman, desperate to find a companion for his journey, appeals, first to Fellowship, then to Kindred, and finally to Cousin to join him, but all three refuse. And here the audience begins to feel the bite of the double-edged weapon that allegory provides. For Everyman becomes at one and the same time a moral symbol for all mankind, and a human individual revealing the psychology of a man conscious that the mark of death is upon him. Seen in the light of his symbolical role, Everyman teaches the lesson of the frailty, transitoriness and wastefulness of man's most cherished worldly experiences, while his impact as a person reflects the feeling of horror and sadness in a dying man who clings desperately to life. So cunningly wrought is the theme of the play that it is rarely possible to separate the symbolical and moral from the physical and psychological. It is upon the last two, however, that the theatrical pathos of the play mainly depends.

The fourth figure or abstraction to whom Everyman makes an appeal is Goods. But Goods (Wealth) chides Everyman. Is he so foolish as to think that his wealth has been given him for ever? No, it was only lent to him: and in any case, how has Everyman employed his riches? Has he with justice and moderation shared them with the poor? He has not done so, with the result that the book of reckoning which he must carry with him on his journey is blotted and smudged.

This brings us to a point which is almost exactly mid-way through the play, by which time Everyman is revealed stripped of friends, relatives and wealth. The call of Death has reduced all such worldly treasures to uselessness and irrelevance. Everyman feels the loneliness that is the inescapable truth which we all have to face. What follows in the play concerns the personal virtues and faculties of the lonely Everyman and his desperate struggle for salvation. Thus we see a natural division of the action of *Everyman*

107

into two almost exactly equal parts. The perfect symmetry of the play's construction is not the least of its beauties.

Everyman now calls upon Good Deeds but finds that she is too weak to stand on her feet. Knowing that he must depend upon the pleading of his Good Deeds at the Final Reckoning, Everyman stands confounded until Good Deeds urges him to seek the advice of her sister, Knowledge. The words of Knowledge as she makes her entry have become immortal:

> Everyman, I will go with thee, and be thy guide,
> In thy most need to go by thy side.

From this point forward Everyman acts in the light of religion. Knowledge conducts him to Confession who introduces Everyman to the rigours of penitential discipline. As Everyman scourges himself Good Deeds slowly gains strength and rises to her feet. Everyman, having put on the robe of contrition, is joined by Discretion, Strength, Five Wits and Beauty, and is now ready to receive the last sacrament of the dying. This was the final act of cleansing from sin without which the soul could not be saved from the jaws of Hell. To the mediaeval mind, as to many modern minds, to die without this last ministration was and is an appallingly terrifying prospect. We must therefore regard this point in the play as a solemn climax. There is a brief pause in the action as Everyman leaves the stage for this purpose, and the time is occupied in an especially interesting way by Knowledge who makes a speech in praise of the sacrament and of the priesthood. This speech is a vivid reflection of the religious turmoil of the fifteenth century in which the powers of the priesthood were being subjected to furious argument, and it is significant that Knowledge, supported by Five Wits, should be given the task of defending the priesthood, and at the same time of condemning the loose living of bad priests.

On the return of Everyman to the stage, all is ready for his approach to the grave and the closing episode of the play. And here we are able to see most clearly the acute horror with which the mediaeval mind contemplated the physical corruption of death and the firmly disciplined faith with which it accepted the 'Doom' that lay beyond.

As Everyman stands before the grave he addresses Beauty in words of the deepest pathos:

Everyman
For into this cave must I creep
And turn to earth, and there to sleep.

Beauty
What! into this grave? Alas!

Everyman
Yea, there shall ye consume,
   more or less*.

[*no matter whether you are great or humble.]*

Beauty
And what! should I smother here?

Everyman
Yea, by my faith, and never more appear.
In this world live no more we shall,
But in heaven before the highest Lord of all.

And Beauty, horrified, bows out, to be followed in turn by Strength, Discretion and Five Wits who leave Everyman alone with his Good Deeds.

The whole of the grave scene is extremely moving, especially when seen in action. For while it throws the spiritual message of Christianity into the strongest possible relief, it yet portrays the stark reality of death and the grave. Its religious message is unwavering and pitiless, but in its portrait of man at the moment of his dying it manages to reflect the deep pathos of his helplessness, just as the *Castle of Perseverance* succeeds in doing at the moment of man's birth.

When Knowledge stands alone by the grave to hear the angelic voice welcoming Everyman into Heaven, the clear incisive 'statement' of this great Morality play is brought to an end.

In one particularly important sense the play of *Everyman* marks the end of a theatrical era. As a Morality play it set out to express and defend the simple, uncritical approach to life and Christianity which was so clearly a major feature of the mediaeval culture. As a work of art it was a model of its kind, disciplined, almost to a point of severity, in maintaining its allegory and the stern lines of its conflict. So much was it a culminating point of its age that it is apt to leave one with the feeling that there was nothing more to be said. It takes a very great play to bring about that result.

There are two further plays which need to be mentioned briefly before we bring this book to a close. The first of these is the *Mary*

Magdalene which was probably written at about the same time as the *Castle of Perseverance*.

Strictly speaking, the *Mary Magdalene* is not a Morality play, but a Saint's play devoted to the legendary story of this saint. All the same it has many features of the Morality play, including the allegorical representation of certain of its characters. It is very long, and is divided into two parts which obviously call for two distinct performances. The first part deals with the fall of Mary into a life of loose morals, her miraculous conversion and her return to her home in the Castle of Maudleyn (Magdalene). The second part deals with Mary's journey to the country of Marcylle and her conversion of its King and Queen.

It is the treatment of Mary's 'fall' that invites our special attention because of its curious blending of the allegorical with the worldly or realistic. In the course of the action Satan plots with the allegorical characters of the World and the Seven Deadly Sins to corrupt the soul of Mary after the death of her father, Cyrus. They lay siege in true allegorical manner to the Castle of Maudleyn where Mary sits in a state of acute mourning. Lechery gains entrance to the castle and, stealing in upon Mary, enters into conversation with her. With cunning references to the young woman's beauty, and subtle arguments upon the self-deception of grief, he tempts her into leaving the castle to enjoy the attractions of the City of Jerusalem—a typical case of 'drowning one's sorrows'.

On arrival in Jerusalem Lechery conducts Mary to a tavern where the taverner introduces her to the delights of wine. A young gallant enters whose name is Curiosity, and Lechery immediately advises Mary that here is the man to revive her spirits. Mary falls into the trap, and the following dialogue takes place:

> *Mary*
> Call him in taverner, as ye my love will have;
> And we shall make full merry if he will abide.
>
> *Taverner*
> How, how, my Master Curiosity!
>
> *Curiosity*
> What is your will, sir? What will ye with me?
>
> *Taverner*
> Here are gentlewomen desire your presence to see,
> And for to drink with you this tide.

Curiosity (advancing to Mary)
Ah, dear duchess, my desire's eye!
Resplendent of colour, most of femininity,
Your sovereign colours set with sincerity!
Consider my love in-to yower alye*   [*Take my love into
Or else I am smitten with pains   your alliance]
   of perplexity.

As one might expect, Curiosity manages to seduce Mary without much difficulty, and there is untold joy on the stage of the World where the World, the Flesh and Satan are assembled.

Now, what is so striking about the play up to this point is the tendency to present allegorical figures as distinct human types. This is most clearly apparent in the tavern scene in which Curiosity introduces himself as a foppish young gallant, over-dressed, sexually eager and 'wolfish'. The taverner is, of course, true to life, while Mary becomes transformed into a giddy-headed young virgin 'asking for trouble' and an easy prey to any would-be seducer. The scene is highly effective within the context of the play, but there is something more which forces itself upon our attention. We have only to take the scene out of its context to find that it would fit remarkably well into a Victorian melodrama in which a foolish and unsophisticated young virgin is seduced by a plausible, unscrupulous and sexually experienced man. There is a moral to be gathered by those who choose to look for it but the impact is critical and social. In this respect the scene looks away from our concept of mediaeval theatre towards an age which was to use its stage to focus the attention of its audience upon the struggles of men and women in the conflicts of this world rather than the Christian conflict for the redemption of men's souls.

The impression of change in theatrical concepts is given to us even more strongly by the play of *Mankind* which was also written before the end of the fifteenth century. The play was performed as a morality, though it had little to do with morals, social or otherwise. We might more reasonably describe it as a bawdy lark or farce built upon the pattern of a Morality play. Historically, however, the play is exceptionally interesting for a number of reasons. In the first place, it was performed by a company of wandering players who took a collection of money from the audience. Secondly, it provides evidence to suggest that it was written for performance in an inn-yard. Finally, although all

111

the characters bear the symbolical names proper to allegory, they are all consciously drawn as true-to-life types.

What impresses us most, perhaps, about *Mankind* is the fact that it reveals all the characteristics of a professional 'show'. If its tone is bawdy, and its action rough and violent, which they are, then it is because the play was professionally aimed at people whose tastes tended strongly in similar directions—which they did. Hence the mockery to which the Morality pattern was reduced.

We need not describe the plot in any detail. Superficially it is true to type. Mankind is subjected to the conflict between good and evil influences. He is obedient at first to the former, but then succumbs to the latter, only to repent and find salvation. We soon discover, however, that no serious lesson is intended, for Mercy, who is the only 'good' influence, bears all the characteristics of a long-winded priest, while Mankind is presented as a simple, gullible tiller of the soil whose lack of wit makes him an obvious target for any practical joker who comes in his way. And practical jokers there are in the characters of Mischief, New-Gyse (New-fangledness), Now-A-Days (Be-With-It), Nought (Naughty) and Titivillus (the Devil) who collectively, and perhaps rather unfairly, represent the powers of Hell, though in reality they are pretty fair characterizations of hooligans and rogues.

With such characters as these in mind we may easily imagine the style of entertainment offered by the play. Mercy is pitilessly teased, as is Mankind, who in sheer exasperation attacks his tormentors with his spade, laying about him lustily and occasionally thrusting them in their private parts. Titivillus—evidently a favourite attraction since his appearance is deliberately delayed until the collection has been taken—avenges his faithful followers by placing a board beneath the soil which Mankind is about to dig. And so riotous action continues, interrupted here and there with a bawdy song which might bring blushes to the faces even of a modern rugby club.

The play of *Mankind* was a 'local' play, intended for performance around the towns and villages of East Anglia and the Fens, as we know from allusions to various places in the text. Thus does the play enter into history as an example of popular entertainment specially written for a company of strolling players: professional 'vagabonds' who were to forge such strong links in the chain of events which led to the great theatre of the Elizabethans. As we have seen, despite its high-sounding name, its connection with the Christian tradition which in legend and allegory had saturated mediaeval consciousness was but slight, since the farcical representation of human types was its chief aim. In this it partially reflected a change in audience appeal which had become wholly apparent in France where a theatre of farce directed entirely at social and domestic life was already established. The famous farce of *Pierre Pathelin* which was written about 1470 and which is still performed, provides us with evidence of the extent to which the art of farce had progressed in France by this time.

As for the use of the stage as a pulpit in serious drama, this was to continue well beyond the middle of the sixteenth century. But whenever it was so used, its conflict related to the personal opinions of men in the fury of religious controversy rather than the abstractions of sin and virtue as the mediaeval world understood them. In other words, the mediaeval concept of the soul as the point of conflict between the powers of Heaven and Hell was giving way to the individual opinions of men as to what was morally good and bad in themselves and in others. The Devil, when he appeared, was usually an object of fun.

The same changes in human outlook, particularly in England, were to affect the Miracle plays as much as they did the Moralities: not in their form, but in their popularity. They continued to be acted well into the sixteenth century—there are records of their performance early in the following century—but their appeal began to wane in the storm of religious argument. They were, moreover, coming to be regarded as a rustic, unsophisticated kind of theatrical entertainment, not to be compared with the high flights of fancy and inventiveness which were beginning to take the stage in the new age which we call the Renaissance.

There was nothing sudden in the transition from the old mediaeval theatrical culture to the new, as the appearance of *Everyman* towards the end of the fifteenth century will testify. Revolutions in the human arts do not take place all that quickly. A period which was far from inspiring had to elapse before the New Age could involve the people in a new, popular theatre. When, during the second half of the sixteenth century, it did so, the theatre that resulted was most glorious. But the evolution of the theatre of the Tudors and the Elizabethans is a different story altogether.

GLOSSARY OF TERMS

anthem	a song, usually of exultation, thanksgiving or praise
antiphony	the singing of alternate verses of a song or psalm by two evenly divided parts of a choir or chorus
burlesque	the turning of what we usually regard as the normal order of things upside-down or 'topsy-turvy'
catharsis	a sudden release from tension which may be either physical or emotional: in the theatre a 'catharsis point' is reached when the audience experiences a sudden feeling of release from the tension of tragedy or comedy—in the latter case the release would probably express itself in an explosion of laughter
chorus or **choir**	in its original or ritualistic sense, a group of performers in song and/or dance, trained to lead and represent an audience or congregation rather than entertain them
cosmic	that which has to do with the universe and not merely with the earth: cosmic drama, therefore, is concerned with the fate of the universe—its beginning and its end
farce	the projection of what we usually regard as normal to abnormal or absurd proportions either through parody or 'farcical' situation
hubris	the ignoring—usually through over-confidence or pride—of the uncertainties of fate or destiny
liturgy	the form prescribed or laid down for the observance of religious ritual
misericord	a shelf or subsidiary seat fixed beneath the main seat of a choir stall, upon which monks or members of the clergy could rest while remaining in a semi-standing position; these were often elaborately carved

Mosaic Law the ancient law of the Jews as represented in the first five books of the Old Testament (the *Pentateuch*)

precentor in mediaeval churches the ruler and, sometimes, leading singer (cantor) of the chorus or choir

proscenium arch the arch forming the frame of the 'picture stage' in a proscenium theatre

theatre a word frequently used in two quite distinct senses the first of which is physical while the other is abstract, denoting a quality. In the physical sense a theatre is *any* place in which action may be seen or demonstrated. In the abstract sense 'theatre' is a ritualistic quality usually denoting the power of a play to bring about a common reaction in an audience. When used in this sense 'theatre' is closely related to the 'feeling of belonging' in an audience

Vespers the service of Vespers takes place in the early evening and forms a part of the Canonical Office, which is the name given to the order of divine worship throughout the day

BOOK LIST

THE DRAMA AND THE STAGE

Chambers, Sir E. K., *The Mediaeval Stage*, Vols I and II, Oxford Univ. Press, 1903

Chambers, Sir E. K., *English Literature at the Close of the Middle Ages—* Essay I, *'Mediaeval Drama'*, Oxford Univ. Press, 1945

Craig, H., *English Religious Drama of the Middle Ages*, Oxford Univ. Press, 1955

Frank, G., *The Mediaeval French Drama*, Oxford Univ. Press, 1954

Hardison, O. B., *Christian Drama in the Middle Ages*, John Hopkins Press, Baltimore, 1965

Kinghorn, A. M., *Medieval Drama*, Cambridge Univ. Press

Kolve, V. A., *The Play Called Corpus Christi*, Stanford Univ. Press, 1966

Mantzius, K., *A History of Theatrical Art*, Vol. II, Duckworth, 1903

Nicoll, Allardyce, *Masks, Mimes and Miracles*, Harrap, 1931

Rossiter, A. P., *English Drama from Early Times to the Elizabethans*, Hutchinson, 1950

Salter, F. M., *Mediaeval Drama in Chester*, Toronto Univ. Press, 1955

Southern, R., *The Mediaeval Theatre in the Round*, Faber & Faber, 1957

Ward, A. W., *A History of English Dramatic Literature to the Death of Queen Anne*, Vol. I, London, 1899

Wickham, Glynne, *Early English Stages*, Vol. I, Routledge & Kegan Paul, 1966

Wickham, Glynne, *The Mediaeval Theatre*, Weidenfeld & Nicolson, 1974

Young, Karl, *The Drama of the Medieval Church*, Oxford Univ. Press, 1933

TEXTS OF PLAYS

The York Plays, Toulmin-Smith, L., Oxford Univ. Press

The Chester Plays (2 vols), Deimling and Matthews, Early English Text Society

The Coventry Corpus Christi Plays, Hardin Craig, Early English Text Society

The Towneley Plays, England and Pollard, Early English Text Society

Ludus Coventriae or The Plaie called Corpus Christi, Black, K. S., Early English Text Society

Non-Cycle Plays and Fragments [Contains the Shrewsbury Fragments, The Norwich Grocers' Play, The Newcastle Play, The Northampton *Abraham*, The Brome *Abraham*, The Play of the Sacrament, *The Pride of Life, Dux Moraud*, and other fragments] Davis, N., Early English Text Society

The Macro Plays [*The Castle of Perseverance, Wisdom, Mankind*], Eccles, M., Early English Text Society

The Digby Plays [*The Conversion of St. Paul, St Mary Magdalen, The Massacre of Innocents and Purification*] Furnivall, F. J., Early English Text Society

Le Mystère d'Adam [text in Norman French and Latin] Studer, P., Manchester University Press

Chief Pre-Shakespearean Dramas [Includes an invaluable selection of Latin plays with English translations], Adams, J. Q., Harrap

English Miracle Plays, Moralities and Interludes [Includes the York *Creation* and *Fall of Lucifer*; *Noah's Flood* and *The Sacrifice of Isaac* (Chester); *The Second Shepherds' Play* (Towneley); *The Salutation and Conception* (N Town); *Mary Magdalen* (shortened version); *The Castle of Perseverance* (shortened version); *Everyman* (shortened version); and the following interludes: John Rastell's *The Four Elements*; Skelton's *Magnyfycence*; Heywood's *The Pardoner and the Frere*; *Thersytes*; Bale's *King John*], Pollard, A. W., Oxford University Press

Three Mediaeval Plays (*The Coventry Nativity Play, Everyman, Master Pierre Pathelin*), Allen, J., Heinemann

Everyman: with other Interludes and Miracle Plays [Includes *Everyman*; *God's Promises*; *The Deluge*; *The Sacrifice of Isaac* (Chester); *The Second Shepherds' Play*; *The Crucifixion*; *The Harrowing of Hell* (Towneley); *The Three Maries* (Cornish)], Everyman's Library, Dent

The York Plays (shortened modernized version), Purvis, J. S., Society for the Propagation of Christian Knowledge

117

THE SOCIAL, RELIGIOUS AND ARTISTIC BACKGROUND

Evans, J. (Ed.), *The Flowering of the Middle Ages*, Thames and Hudson

Harris, M. D., *The Coventry Leet Book* (2 vols), Early English Text Society

Hildburgh, W. L., *English Alabaster Carvings as Records of Mediaeval Religious Drama*, Oxford Univ. Press, 1949

Owst, G. R., *Literature and Pulpit in Medieval England*, Cambridge Univ. Press, 1933

Southern, R. W., *Western Society and the Church in the Middle Ages*, Pelican Books, 1970

Toulmin-Smith, L., *English Guilds, their Statutes and Customs*, Early English Text Society

Trevelyan, G. M., *Illustrated Social History*, Vol. I, Longmans, 1949

Warrington, J. (Ed.), *The Paston Letters* (2 vols), Dent (Everyman's Library)

White, B., *The Dance of Death*, Early English Text Society

Ziegler, P., *The Black Death*, Collins, 1969

The Shorter Cambridge Mediaeval History (2 vols), Cambridge Univ. Press

INDEX

by ANN HUGH-JONES

Note The 8-page section of monochrome plates appears between pages 64 and 65. In references to line drawings, the number of the page on which a figure appears is given in brackets after the figure number.